OECD Public Governance Reviews

Building Capacity for Evidence-Informed Policy-Making

LESSONS FROM COUNTRY EXPERIENCES

This work is published under the responsibility of the Secretary-General of the OECD. The opinions expressed and arguments employed herein do not necessarily reflect the official views of OECD member countries.

This document, as well as any data and map included herein, are without prejudice to the status of or sovereignty over any territory, to the delimitation of international frontiers and boundaries and to the name of any territory, city or area.

The statistical data for Israel are supplied by and under the responsibility of the relevant Israeli authorities. The use of such data by the OECD is without prejudice to the status of the Golan Heights, East Jerusalem and Israeli settlements in the West Bank under the terms of international law.

Note by Turkey
The information in this document with reference to "Cyprus" relates to the southern part of the Island. There is no single authority representing both Turkish and Greek Cypriot people on the Island. Turkey recognises the Turkish Republic of Northern Cyprus (TRNC). Until a lasting and equitable solution is found within the context of the United Nations, Turkey shall preserve its position concerning the "Cyprus issue".

Note by all the European Union Member States of the OECD and the European Union
The Republic of Cyprus is recognised by all members of the United Nations with the exception of Turkey. The information in this document relates to the area under the effective control of the Government of the Republic of Cyprus.

Please cite this publication as:
OECD (2020), *Building Capacity for Evidence-Informed Policy-Making: Lessons from Country Experiences*, OECD Public Governance Reviews, OECD Publishing, Paris, *https://doi.org/10.1787/86331250-en*.

ISBN 978-92-64-53757-6 (print)
ISBN 978-92-64-47315-7 (pdf)

OECD Public Governance Reviews
ISSN 2219-0406 (print)
ISSN 2219-0414 (online)

Photo credits: Cover © Andrii Symonenko/Shutterstock.com.

Corrigenda to publications may be found on line at: *www.oecd.org/about/publishing/corrigenda.htm*.
© OECD 2020

The use of this work, whether digital or print, is governed by the Terms and Conditions to be found at *http://www.oecd.org/termsandconditions*.

Foreword

Governments are facing growing pressures to deliver public services to citizens in a complex, fragmented and unpredictable environment. Evidence-informed policy-making can play a crucial role in designing, implementing and delivering better public policies. However, effectively connecting evidence and policy-making remains a challenge. Institutional gaps, insufficient skills and capacity, and a lack of an effective knowledge-brokering function are common barriers to the use of evidence in policy-making. A failure to act on evidence about which polices work, which do not, and why, is an inefficient use of resources. Therefore, increasing government's capacity for an evidence-informed approach to policy-making is an essential part of good public governance.

The report focuses on the skills and capacities governments need to strengthen evidence-informed policy-making, including issues of staff capability, in terms of psychological and physical capacity, knowledge and skills, motivation and opportunity in terms of the external factors that prompt an individual to make use of evidence. The report identifies tools, strategies and possible interventions governments can use at the individual, organisational and institutional level. In terms of the individual skills, the report identifies the skills to understand, obtain, interrogate and assess, use and apply evidence; as well as the capacity to engage with stakeholders and evaluate the success of evidence-informed policy-making.

Beyond individual skills, the report also analyses the capacity for uptake of evidence-informed decision making at the organisational level, in terms of the institutional, strategic and human resource management aspects. Finally, the report considers the wider capacity of the public sector to facilitate an evidence-driven management and decision-making culture. On all these dimensions, the report offers concrete examples and highlights the role of institutions, organisations and leadership.

This work was undertaken in the context of the OECD work on fostering evidence-informed policy-making as part of the activities of the Public Governance Committee for 2019-20 and benefited from collaboration with the European Union Joint Research Centre.

Strengthening capacity for use and demand of evidence remains a work in progress in many jurisdictions. But it is also an essential element for maintaining citizens' trust in decision-making processes across public institutions.

Acknowledgements

This report was prepared in the OECD Directorate for Public Governance (GOV) under the leadership of Marcos Bonturi, Director, and Martin Forst, head of GOV's Governance Reviews and Partnerships Division.

The report was drafted by Daniel Acquah, policy analyst at the OECD at the time of drafting, under the strategic direction of Stephane Jacobzone, Head of Unit for evidence, monitoring and policy evaluation. Danielle Mulima, Katarzina Lisek and Lizeth Fuquene contributed sections and provided highly valuable research assistance. Editorial and production support was provided by Ciara Muller and Amelia Godber.

The authors are grateful to the European Commission Joint Research Centre for the collaboration on building capacity for evidence-informed policy-making. In particular, the OECD would like to thank David Mair and Milena Raykovska who co-organised the workshop 'Skills for Policymakers for Evidence – Informed Policy-making,' which took place in April 2018 and which was co-opened by Charlina Vitcheva, Deputy Director-General of the Joint Research Centre. Within the OECD Secretariat, Raquel Paramo and Javier Gonzalez provided assistance for the workshop.

The authors are also grateful to many of the participating experts who have contributed to the work, including Eeva Hellstrom (SITRA, Finland), Ulla Rosenstrom (Prime Minister's Office Finland), Rozenn Desplatz (France), Kasey Treadwell Shine (Ireland), Lynette Sing (South Africa), Jen Gold (UK), Tatjana Verrier (EC), Françoise Waintrop (ENA, France), Carrie Exton (OECD), Diana Epstein (US), Ulrik Mogensen (EC), Elena Oyon (Alliance for Useful Evidence), Wim Rietdijk (the Netherlands), Nick Carrol (New Zealand), Annelise Dennis (INASP), Jakob Wegener Friis (EC), Charlotte Hall (Sweden), Antonio López Soto (Spain), Frank Zwetsloot (Science Works/Netherlands), Jonas Fischer (EC).

The report received detailed and comprehensive feedback from the Public Governance Committee and the authors are grateful to country officials for all the feedback and additional material. Finally, the authors wish to acknowledge the feedback received from Daniel Gerson, Edwin Lau, Natalia Nolan, Toni Rumpf and Ernesto Soria Morales in the OECD Public Governance Directorate.

Table of contents

Foreword 3

Acknowledgements 5

Executive Summary 9

1 Building capacity for evidence-informed policy-making: the need to connect supply with demand for evidence 11
Contemporary policy challenges 12
The contribution of evidence-informed policy-making to good public governance 12
Effective connections between evidence and policy-making remain elusive 14
Acknowledging the importance of cognitive constraints and biases 14
A focus on the demand side 15
References 16

2 The contribution of existing work on the intersection of evidence and policy-making 19
Related OECD work 20
Contribution from the European Commission Joint Research Centre 21
References 22

3 What capacities and skills are needed for EIPM? 23
Increasing the use of evidence depends on capability, motivation and opportunity 24
Addressing capacity at multiple levels 25
References 28
Note 29

4 What interventions, strategies and tools can strengthen capacity for EIPM? 31
Identifying barriers and facilitators 32
How can governments identify and select appropriate strategies? 32
Diagnostic tools to promote understanding of evidence 33
Initiatives to increase policy-makers' ability to obtain evidence 35
Improving policy-makers' capacity to interrogate, assess, use and apply evidence 37
Mentoring initiatives to build policy-makers' capacity to use evidence 42
Initiatives to promote engagement and interaction between policy-makers and suppliers of evidence 43
Diagnostic tools to evaluate organisational capacities for EIPM 49
Initiatives to build organisational capacities for evidence-informed policy-making 51
References 62

Note 66

5 Conclusion 67
Recommendations 68
Future work 70
References 71
Note 71

Annex A. Mapping of interventions, strategies and tools onto the skills framework for EIPM 73

Figures
Figure 2.1. Skills for a high performing civil service 20
Figure 2.2. Core Skills for Public Sector Innovation 21
Figure 3.1. The Capability Opportunity Motivation -Behaviour model 24
Figure 3.2. A model for increasing the use of evidence by policy-makers at multiple levels 25
Figure 3.3. The Skillset for Evidence-informed Policy-making 26
Figure 4.1. Barriers and Facilitators to EIPM 32
Figure 4.2. Mapping existing initiatives against the OECD/JRC skills framework 33
Figure 4.3. Seeking, Engaging with and Evaluating Research (SEER) 34

Follow OECD Publications on:

 http://twitter.com/OECD_Pubs

 http://www.facebook.com/OECDPublications

 http://www.linkedin.com/groups/OECD-Publications-4645871

 http://www.youtube.com/oecdilibrary

 http://www.oecd.org/oecddirect/

Executive Summary

This report analyses the skills and capacities governments need to strengthen evidence-informed policy-making and identifies a range of possible interventions governments can use, based on country good practice. Evidence-informed policy-making can be defined as a process whereby multiple sources of information, including statistics, data and the best available research evidence and evaluations, are consulted before making a decision to plan, implement, and (where relevant) alter public policies and programmes. This report adopts a broad definition of evidence to mean a systematic investigative process to increase or revise current knowledge that encompasses policy evaluation as well as scientific investigations.

Increasing governments' capacity for an evidence-informed approach to policy-making is a critical part of fostering good public governance to achieve broad societal goals, such as promoting sustainable development or improving well-being. This requires both investing in skills for the use of evidence by policy-makers and senior officials working at the political-administrative interface and taking systemic approaches to building capacity for evidence-informed policy-making in the public sector. The goal is an agile and responsive government that is well equipped to address complex policy challenges.

Despite the potential benefits, an effective connection between the supply and the demand for evidence in the policy-making process often remains elusive. Many governments lack the necessary infrastructure to build such connections. This report looks at how government and the public sector can support senior officials, experts and advisors working at the political/administrative interface and in the policy-making process. It focuses on how to build capacity on the demand side of evidence, as this issue has received less attention to date than the supply of evidence.

The report highlights good practices for enhancing the collective skill set for evidence-informed policy-making. Improving governments' capacity for an evidence-informed approach will require scaling up the full range of skills for using evidence, as well as engaging with stakeholders and evaluating success.

The report then presents actions, tools and strategies governments can use to build their capacity in this area. These include diagnostic tools to understand the range of existing capacities and ensure that interventions are well matched to governments' needs. The report also presents initiatives designed to increase policy-makers' ability to access and obtain evidence. Existing country practices comprise a range of initiatives to improve individual policy-makers' capacity to use evidence, including both senior civil service leadership programmes and more intensive skills development programmes for the broader civil service. Mentoring is another approach that can be used to support individual capacity building, by giving personalised guidance in relation to 'real-world' application of knowledge. Different strategies for promoting interaction and engagement between suppliers of evidence and policy-makers are reviewed. Such interaction can help to build trusted relationships and increase opportunities for research to affect policy-making. These approaches include one-off or periodic forums, various platforms for ongoing interactivity and more intensive partnership projects.

Beyond individual skills, promoting the use of evidence requires more systematic and organisational approaches. The shared goal of interventions to build organisational structures and systems is to embed research use and drive a culture of evidence use within policy organisations. Improving capacity includes strategies such as improving organisational infrastructure, tools, resources and processes; workforce development; and establishing strategic units to support an evidence-informed approach across government.

The recommendations below should assist governments in building their capacity for evidence-informed policy-making:

- Capacity-building initiatives need to consider the local political and institutional context of research use.
- This implies acquiring an understanding of the often messy reality of how actual policy-making occurs, and how and when to seize the opportunities for evidence to play a role. This can be particularly important in a context of shifting political priorities where governments can be confronted with citizens' anger and lack of trust in public institutions.
- Capacity-building initiatives need to address the full range of skills that influence the use of evidence, including skills for understanding, obtaining, interrogating and assessing, using and applying evidence, as well as engaging with stakeholders and evaluating success.
- To enable change, organisations first need to gather information on current capacities, the desire for change, and existing barriers and facilitators of evidence use within the system. Based on the analysis of capacity gaps, organisations need to identify the right kind of skills that are needed to then focus the most suitable interventions.
- Institutions, organisational structures and systems enable the effective use of evidence – without addressing these, initiatives are unlikely to succeed.
- Building capacity for evidence use requires systemic and institutional approaches. These include strengthening organisational tools, resources and processes, investing in basic infrastructure, including data management systems and knowledge brokers, and establishing strategic units to champion an evidence-based approach. Mandates, legislation and regulation are also important tools to facilitate the use of evidence.
- Strategic leadership is critical to drive the organisational change necessary for improved evidence-informed policy-making.
- Embedding evidence-informed approaches in policy-making requires strategic and committed leadership, for example from the centre of government, or from units with a mandate for delivering the programme of government. An evidence-informed approach can also be leveraged through performance-driven approaches to resource allocation, and can rely on high-profile positions with a crosscutting mission across departments.
- Capacity-building initiatives should embed evaluation from the beginning to inform the implementation process and support continuous learning and improvement.
- It is important to reduce the knowledge gap to assess what are the most effective initiatives that help to foster evidence use throughout the public sector and find ways to measure impact.
- Capacity-building initiatives need to be embedded within organisational structures and strategies to enable sustainable and long-term change.
- Evidence-informed policy-making requires more than short-term and short-lived initiatives. Fully embedding them inside government activity may require stronger regulatory or legislative anchors, as well as structural integration in public sector processes to prevent such initiatives from being "washed out" after an initial period of enthusiasm.

1 Building capacity for evidence-informed policy-making: the need to connect supply with demand for evidence

This chapter discusses the need to connect supply with demand of evidence in a complex political context characterised by a global over-supply of knowledge. The chapter discusses the contribution that evidence-informed policy-making can make to good public governance, which requires building new skills and capacity in the public sector. There is a need to address the elusive connections between evidence and policy-making, while acknowledging the importance of cognitive constraints and bias. This highlights the rationale for focusing on the demand of evidence, at the level of individual skills, as well as at the structural and organisational levels.

Contemporary policy challenges

Ensuring demand for evidence has become very challenging in a context of global over-supply of knowledge and the complex political process. The amount of information to be considered by policy-makers is overwhelming and ever more complex, while the individual and organisational capacity to process information can be restricted and skewed by biases. Simultaneously, important evidence gaps remain on 'what works' in many policy areas. As a result, moving the frontiers of evidence, policy and people for joint solutions involves difficult trade-offs just at a time when evidence-informed policies are very much needed. These challenges are compounded in a "post-truth" world, where the speed of reaction is dictated by a wide variety of media and where 'facts' may be presented without foundation or verification. Governments are also facing citizens' anger, and political forces are responding to citizens' perceptions in ways that may challenge some of the established arrangements. Maintaining the capacity of government to deliver in effective ways that respond to political priorities without prejudgement is critical to respond to these new challenges.

This requires building new skills and capacity in the public sector. The challenge is to be able to foster informed judgement and to ensure that the public sector is equipped with the right skill-set to nurture evidence-informed policy-making (EIPM). New technologies and new possibilities with data analytics, a growing body of policy-relevant research and a diversity of citizen perspectives demand new skills for effective and timely policy-making.

Those interested in serving the public interest need the right skills to commission, understand and integrate evidence. Effective civil service capacity support should ideally encompass a range of interventions: from developing skills, values and norms to promote EIPM at an individual level, to supporting the adoption of procedures, incentives and resources (financial and human) to enhance use of evidence. The civil service, particularly the Senior Civil Service, needs critical appraisal skills in order to assess the provenance of evidence, its robustness, its relevance and impact, and at the same time meet ethical standards, while feeding into institutional set-ups that take into account wider political constraints.

The contribution of evidence-informed policy-making to good public governance

Evidence has a critical role to play in improving the quality, responsiveness and accessibility of public services. It can play a role throughout the key stages of the policy cycle and is increasingly recognised as a critical part of good governance. Evidence-informed policy-making can be defined as a process whereby multiple sources of information, including statistics, data and including the best available research evidence and evaluations, are consulted before making a decision to plan, implement, and (where relevant) alter public policies, programmes and deliver quality public other services. '(derived from (Langer, Tripney and Gough, 2016[1]; OECD, 2018[2]). This report adopts a correspondingly broad definition of research evidence to mean 'a systematic investigative process employed to increase or revise current knowledge' (Langer, Tripney and Gough, 2016[1]) that encompasses policy evaluation as well as scientific investigations.

Policy design benefits from 'policy memory', an understanding of what challenges have been experienced in the past and what previous good practices could be incorporated into the current reform effort. This underlines the importance of thorough stock taking of the existing evidence base to inform policy and programme design.

Evidence synthesis, such as systematic reviews, helps to prevent one-sided policy design, avoid duplication and ensure scarce resources are directed at areas of policy requiring further solutions. Evidence synthesis also helps to identify policies and practices that have been found to be ineffective, where caution should be exercised before further investment in the absence of further refinement and testing (Gough, Oliver and Thomas, 2013[3]; Torgerson and Torgerson, 2003[4]).

Evidence also has a critical contribution to make in policy implementation, which requires significant planning and management support. Implementation science provides an understanding of how to adapt policies to meet local needs, whilst guarding against changes that may affect outcomes: this can make the difference between a successful implementation of an intervention and one that is ineffective or potentially even harmful (Moore, Bumbarger and Cooper, 2013[5]). Gathering evidence on factors that help and hinder implementation also facilitates dissemination of effective interventions at scale and achieve outcomes at the population level (Castro, Barrera and Holleran Steiker, 2010[6]).

Policy evaluation is also critical to understand why some (complex) policies work and why others do not. As one important source of policy relevant knowledge, policy evaluation supports policy choices rooted in an evidence-informed policy-making process. Solid policy evaluation and its strategic use throughout the policy cycle can foster a range of objectives such as policies' effectiveness, value for money, accountability and overall transparency of a policy-making process (OECD, 2018). Building evaluation capacity is an important component of international aid towards development, which are subject to strong accountability objectives and it also enables governments to assess how policies stimulate progress towards the Sustainable Development Goals (SDGs).

When used systematically and as a system-wide approach, regulatory impact analysis (RIA) is a critical tool to ensure greater quality of a particular type of government intervention, which concerns the use of regulatory and legislative tools (OECD, 2018[2]). RIA is an important tool to address the issue that government interventions do not always fully consider their likely effects at the time of their development. As a result, there are many instances of embarrassment, unintended consequences and ultimately negative impacts for citizens, businesses and society as a whole that could be better identified through a RIA process (OECD, 2018[2]). Carefully designed and executive RIA, undertaken at the inception of policy proposals ensures informed judgements can be made between policy options.

While this report starts from the premise that evidence-informed policy-making can lead to better outcomes, it also acknowledges the inherently complex conditions of the policy-making process, which necessitates multiple approaches to ensure sound public governance. Political decision makers are considering many sources and forms of input including economic, ideological, social and political factors (Newman, Fisher and Shaxson, 2012[7]) and are listening to citizens and other stakeholder groups in order to make decisions in a timely manner. Alongside the civil service, ministerial advisors can also help government leaders in these areas. OECD's Ministerial Advisors Survey (OECD, 2011[8]) finds that advisors have a crucial role to play in helping ministers keep in touch with stakeholders and public opinion in an increasingly complex and fast-paced environment. Evidence will always be mediated through a political process that allows intuition to shape the final policy as part of a democratic process that fully respects political discretion.

There is also a need to address the potential for bias as external voices often try to intervene in the policy-making process to preserve or promote specific interests. As a result, conflicts of interest is another issue that has become a matter of public concern, and that can also impact the quality of evidence and the trust that is attached to it. OECD's 'Guidelines for Managing Conflict of Interest in the Public Service' respond to a growing demand to ensure integrity and transparency in the public sector (OECD, 2003[9]). The primary aim of the Guidelines is to help countries, at central government level, consider Conflict of Interest policy and practice relating to public officials. Demands for transparency in policy-making have also led to concerns over lobbying practices. In 2009, the OECD reviewed the data and experiences of government regulation, legislation and self-regulation, leading to '10 Principles for Transparency and Integrity in Lobbying'. These issues are also pertinent to evidence-informed policy-making and capacity building. The commercialisation of capacity building activities can also create pressure to overstate the benefits, leading to erosion in confidence if expectations are not met (Leadbeater et al., 2018[10]). These wider issues of integrity and transparency of the interface between evidence production and policy-making do matter and need specific attention, even if this goes beyond the scope of the current report.

Effective connections between evidence and policy-making remain elusive

Despite the potential for policies to be based on evidence, in reality an effective connection with many types of research evidence in policy-making remains elusive (Newman, Cherney and Head, 2017[11]). For example, US estimates show that, under the two Obama administrations only 1% of government funding was informed by evidence (Bridgeland and Orszag, 2013[12]). In the UK, there are also concerns about the generation and use of evidence by government. An enquiry into 'missing evidence' found that although UK government spends around 2.5 billion GBP a year on research for policy, only 4 out of 24 departments maintain a database of commissioned research (Sedley, 2016[13]). A report by the National Audit Office on evaluation in government found little systematic information from the government on how it has used the evaluation evidence that it had commissioned or produced (NAO, 2013[14]).

A study of 2,084 public servants in Australia found that although public servants seem to have good access to academic research, they are not using it systematically in crafting policy analysis and advice (Newman, Cherney and Head, 2017[11]). A survey in South Africa also found that while 45% of senior policy-makers intended to use evidence during policy-making, in reality only 9% were able to do this in practice. Policy-makers identify a lack of skill and capacity as one of the reasons why they do not use research and the results of policy evaluation (Campbell et al., 2009[15]; Orton et al., 2011[16]).

One consequence of these challenges is that often, there remains a discrepancy between what is known to be effective as suggested by evidence and what is actually happening in practice on the ground. In health care, where this issue was first identified over two decades ago, it was estimated that overuse, underuse or misuse of health care, failing to take advantage of evidence-based care approaches could cost as much as 91000 deaths per year for chronic conditions, and between 44 000 and 98000 deaths due to preventable medical errors (Kohn LT, 2000[17]). Still today, one salient example of this concerns the importance of handwashing to prevent transmission of infection: a century after the relevant research, there remains chronic underuse of appropriate handwashing in both high-income countries and low to middle-income countries resulting in avoidable illness and deaths (Glasziou et al., 2017[18]). In social services, evidence based interventions for families, which are effective in improving a range of outcomes for children also remain underutilised globally (Kumpfer, Magalhães and Xie, 2017[19]). Underuse of effective interventions represents an inefficient use of resources, causing harm to citizens. Therefore, increasing governments' capacity for an evidence-informed approach remains a critical part of good public governance, to increase the capacity to deliver quality public services and increase citizens' wellbeing in cost effective ways.

Acknowledging the importance of cognitive constraints and biases

While objective evidence is one critical input to the policy-making process, advances in behavioural sciences have demonstrated that decision-making is subject to fundamental constraints and biases. Cognitive biases, ideologies, and competing interests of stakeholders all have the potential to influence the policy-making process. For example, motivated reasoning, the biased assessment of evidence that favours the desired outcome, is a fundamental feature of cognitive reasoning (Mercier and Sperber, 2011[20]; Pennycook and Rand, 2018[21]) This can affect the work of analysts, as well as the approach of senior decision makers and politicians. Time constraints may mean that policymakers use the 'best available' evidence, which includes personal memories that can be most directly accessed by the brain, and previous textbook approaches, rather than waiting for information from the latest scientific experiments and policy evaluations and understanding the complex rationale of some scientific findings.

The OECD is addressing some of the cognitive aspects in work on behavioural insights, to see how to identify the role of psychological bias to design more effective interventions, particularly on the regulatory side (OECD, 2016[22]; OECD, 2017[23]).

The role of cognitive approaches was also fully acknowledged in the OECD's New Approaches to Economic Challenges (NAEC) initiative. NAEC has called for promoting a systemic perspective on interconnected challenges to identify the analytical and policy tools needed to understand them. For example, in 2017, NAEC organised a workshop with experts in the fields of economics, behavioural and cognitive sciences, psychology and philosophy to explore what the study of neuro-economics and neural processes involved in policy-making, to understand those often less understood aspects of human behaviour (OECD, 2017[24]).

This is also an area where the EU Joint Research Centre is currently working to understand and explain the drivers that influence policy-making and political discourse, in order to optimise the way scientific evidence is used in policy-making (European Commission, 2018[25]). This can help to understand how a range of different factors including facts, values, interests and social relations affect the policy-making process, at individual and organisational level.

A focus on the demand side

Building capacity for Evidence-informed policy-making (EIPM), in the public sector will help to implement strategies that aim to increase the efficiency, effectiveness and responsiveness of government, through better use of evidence (Harrow, 2001[26]). This is designed to improve core public governance outcomes, which are impacted by the efficiency, effectiveness and responsiveness of government and of public services. Building capacity for EIPM will help the public sector to engage effectively with the plurality of evidence available in modern global economies. (Newman, Cherney and Head, 2017[11]).

This report intentionally focuses on how to build capacity on the demand side of evidence that is how to generate effective demand and use of evidence. This focus was chosen because there is a lack of research and international comparative examples of how to build capacity on the demand side of evidence-informed policy-making (Newman, Fisher and Shaxson, 2012[7]). This report conceptualises the demand and supply side relationship primarily in terms the civil service/wider public sector and the research and policy profession community, recognising that members of the research and policy profession community can also be situated within government such as economists, statisticians and social researchers.

Nevertheless, this report recognises that evidence-informed policy-making necessitates consideration of both the supply and demand for evidence. A reliable and high-quality supply of policy-relevant evidence is a necessary factor for the use of evidence. While supply of scientific knowledge and of analysis is generally abundant, in many policy areas this supply may be limited or lacking to address specific policy relevant questions. Governments are also recognising that the data they hold is a strategic asset that can used to generate evidence to inform the performance of policies. These supply side issues are addressed in other OECD work, including an upcoming report on the Institutionalisation, Quality and Use of Evaluation (OECD, 2020[27]), as well as an upcoming report on the data driven public sector (OECD, 2019[28]).

This report also addresses the structural and organisational level. A further motivation for building capacity for EIPM in a structural sense is that the majority of work on how to improve evidence use focuses on the *individual* level, such as training courses, linking schemes between policy-makers and training individual researchers or policy-makers to be 'knowledge brokers'. However, a sole focus on individuals places undue expectations on researchers and policy-makers, who may not see it as their role or skills set to transfer knowledge or make use of knowledge (Parkhurst, 2017[29]). A focus on individuals may also limit the potential to generate long-term and system wide change. This is especially true in the context of the 'churn' in employees experienced in the civil service, whether as a result of standard staff rotations or of change of government at senior levels (OECD, 2017[30]).

References

Academies, U. (ed.) (2000), *Building a Safer Health Care System*. [17]

Bridgeland, J. and P. Orszag (2013), *Can Government Play Moneyball? - The Atlantic*, https://www.theatlantic.com/magazine/archive/2013/07/can-government-play-moneyball/309389/ (accessed on 6 December 2018). [12]

Campbell, D. et al. (2009), "Increasing the use of evidence in health policy: practice and views of policy makers and researchers", *Australia and New Zealand Health Policy*, Vol. 6/1, p. 21, http://dx.doi.org/10.1186/1743-8462-6-21. [15]

Castro, F., M. Barrera and L. Holleran Steiker (2010), "Issues and Challenges in the Design of Culturally Adapted Evidence-Based Interventions", *Annual Review of Clinical Psychology*, Vol. 6/1, pp. 213-239, http://dx.doi.org/10.1146/annurev-clinpsy-033109-132032. [6]

European Commission (2018), *Terms of Reference: Expert contributions to the JRC's Enlightenment 2.0 Flagship Report*, European Commission, Brussels, https://ec.europa.eu/jrc/sites/jrcsh/files/enlightenment_termsofreference-expert-contributions_180326.pdf. [25]

Glasziou, P. et al. (2017), "Evidence for underuse of effective medical services around the world", *The Lancet*, Vol. 390/10090, pp. 169-177, http://dx.doi.org/10.1016/S0140-6736(16)30946-1. [18]

Gough, D., S. Oliver and J. Thomas (2013), *Learning from Research: Systematic Reviews for Informing Policy Decisions: A Quick Guide.*. [3]

Harrow, J. (2001), "'CAPACITY BUILDING' AS A PUBLIC MANAGEMENT GOAL - Myth, magic or the main chance?", *Public Management Review*, Vol. 3/2, pp. 209-230, http://dx.doi.org/10.1080/14616670010029593. [26]

Kumpfer, K., C. Magalhães and J. Xie (2017), "Cultural Adaptation and Implementation of Family Evidence-Based Interventions with Diverse Populations", *Prevention Science*, Vol. 18/6, pp. 649-659, http://dx.doi.org/10.1007/s11121-016-0719-3. [19]

Langer, L., J. Tripney and D. Gough (2016), *The science of using science: researching the use of Research evidence in decision-making.*. [1]

Leadbeater, B. et al. (2018), "Ethical Challenges in Promoting the Implementation of Preventive Interventions: Report of the SPR Task Force", *Prevention Science*, pp. 1-13, http://dx.doi.org/10.1007/s11121-018-0912-7. [10]

Mercier, H. and D. Sperber (2011), "Why do humans reason? Arguments for an argumentative theory", *Behavioral and Brain Sciences*, Vol. 34/02, pp. 57-74, http://dx.doi.org/10.1017/S0140525X10000968. [20]

Moore, J., B. Bumbarger and B. Cooper (2013), "Examining Adaptations of Evidence-Based Programs in Natural Contexts", *The Journal of Primary Prevention*, Vol. 34/3, pp. 147-161, http://dx.doi.org/10.1007/s10935-013-0303-6. [5]

NAO (2013), *Evaluation in government*, https://www.nao.org.uk/report/evaluation-government/. [14]

Newman, J., A. Cherney and B. Head (2017), "Policy capacity and evidence-based policy in the public service", *Public Management Review*, Vol. 19/2, pp. 157-174, http://dx.doi.org/10.1080/14719037.2016.1148191. [11]

Newman, K., C. Fisher and L. Shaxson (2012), "Stimulating Demand for Research Evidence: What Role for Capacity-building?", *IDS Bulletin*, Vol. 43/5, pp. 17-24, http://dx.doi.org/10.1111/j.1759-5436.2012.00358.x. [7]

OECD (2020), *Institutionalisation, Quality and Use of Policy Evaluation, Governance Lessons from Countries Experiences*. [27]

OECD (2018), *OECD Best Practice Principles for Regulatory Policy: Regulatory Impact Assessment*, OECD, Paris. [2]

OECD (2017), *Behavioural Insights and Public Policy: Lessons from Around the World*, OECD Publishing, Paris, https://dx.doi.org/10.1787/9789264270480-en. [23]

OECD (2017), *Government at a Glance 2017*, OECD Publishing, http://www.oecd-ilibrary.org/governance/government-at-a-glance-2017_gov_glance-2017-en. [30]

OECD (2017), *The State of Mind in Economics*, http://www.oecd.org/fr/naec/the-state-of-mind-in-economics.htm (accessed on 6 March 2019). [24]

OECD (2016), *Protecting Consumers through Behavioural Insights.*, OECD Publishing. [22]

OECD (2011), *Ministerial Advisors: Role, Influence and Management*, OECD Publishing, Paris, https://dx.doi.org/10.1787/9789264124936-en. [8]

OECD (2003), *RECOMMENDATION OF THE COUNCIL ON GUIDELINES FOR MANAGING CONFLICT OF INTEREST IN THE PUBLIC SERVICE*, http://www.oecd.org/governance/ethics/2957360.pdf (accessed on 3 October 2018). [9]

OECD Publishing, D. (ed.) (2019), *The Path to Becoming a Data-Driven Public Sector,*, http://dx.doi.org/doi.org/10.1787/059814a7-en. [28]

Orton, L. et al. (2011), "The Use of Research Evidence in Public Health Decision Making Processes: Systematic Review", *PLoS ONE*, Vol. 6/7, p. e21704, http://dx.doi.org/10.1371/journal.pone.0021704. [16]

Parkhurst, J. (2017), *The politics of evidence : from evidence-based policy to the good governance of evidence*, Routledge, London, http://researchonline.lshtm.ac.uk/3298900/ (accessed on 23 November 2018). [29]

Pennycook, G. and D. Rand (2018), "Lazy, not biased: Susceptibility to partisan fake news is better explained by lack of reasoning than by motivated reasoning", *Cognition*, http://dx.doi.org/10.1016/J.COGNITION.2018.06.011. [21]

Sedley, S. (2016), *Missing Evidence: Sir Stephen Sedley's inquiry into delayed publication of government commissioned research*, Sense about Science, London, https://www.cloisters.com/news/missing-evidence-sir-stephen-sedley-s-inquiry-into-delayed-publication-of-government-commissioned-research-report-out-now (accessed on 6 December 2018). [13]

Torgerson, C. and D. Torgerson (2003), "The Design and Conduct of Randomised Controlled Trials in Education: Lessons from health care", *Oxford Review of Education*, Vol. 29/1, pp. 67-80, http://dx.doi.org/10.1080/03054980307434. [4]

2 The contribution of existing work on the intersection of evidence and policy-making

This chapter presents the contribution of existing work, including at the OECD, and at European level on the intersection of evidence and policy-making. It introduces the framework of skills for a high performing civil service, as well as the core skills for public sector innovation from the OECD work on public employment and on public sector innovation. It also introduces the framework for skills for evidence-informed policy-making developed by the European Commission Joint Research Centre.

Related OECD work

This work has benefitted from initial work on 'Policy Advisory Systems: Supporting Good Governance and Sound Public Decision Making,' which helped to initiate OECDs work on evidence-informed policy-making. (OECD, 2017[1]).

Building capacity for use of evidence and evaluation in the civil service can also benefit from the broader frameworks developed by the OECD in the context of its work on the civil service in relation to public employment and management on skills. The report on "Skills for a High Performing Civil Service" highlights the critical contribution civil servants make to national growth and prosperity, whilst recognising that global trends such as digitalisation are challenging the public sector to work in new ways (OECD, 2017[2]). Additionally, this report outlines ways in which the public service needs to also be strategic and innovative to adapt to the modern context. This report looks at the capacity and capabilities of civil servants of OECD countries. It explores the skills required to develop better policies and regulations, to work effectively with citizens and service users, to commission cost-effective service delivery, and to collaborate with stakeholders in networked settings (see Figure 2.1). The skills for policy design are those that are most likely to be strengthened by greater capacity for evidence update in the civil service. This previous report offers a framework through which countries can begin to assess the skills they presently have or gaps that may exist. The report also identifies promising trends and innovations in civil service management that can help countries create strategies for their public service.

Figure 2.1. Skills for a high performing civil service

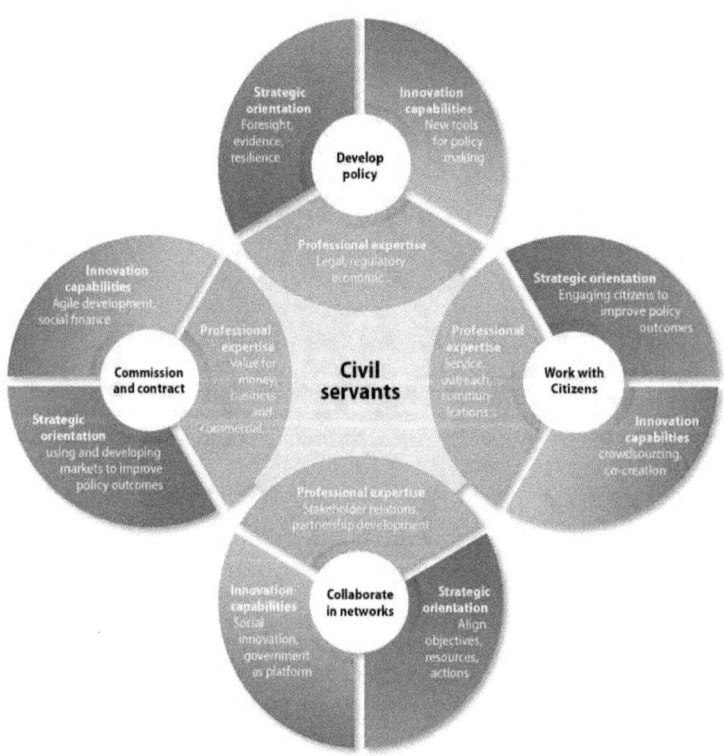

Source: OECD (2017[2])

On the issues related to innovation in civil service management, the report on 'Core Skills for Public Sector Innovation' was prepared in the context of the OECD Observatory on Public Sector Innovation (OECD, 2017[3]). This publication outlines six core skill areas that are designed to support increased levels of innovation in the public sector and increase policy-makers' ability to innovate. These skills include iteration, data literacy, user centricity, curiosity, storytelling and insurgency. These skills allow for innovation through encouraging policy-makers to try new ideas, ensuring that the needs of people are being addressed, that decisions are data-driven and that policy-makers are able to explain the changes that are being made. Some of these skills are also very relevant to build capacity for evidence-informed policy-making, including data literacy and user centricity (See Figure 2.2).

Figure 2.2. Core Skills for Public Sector Innovation

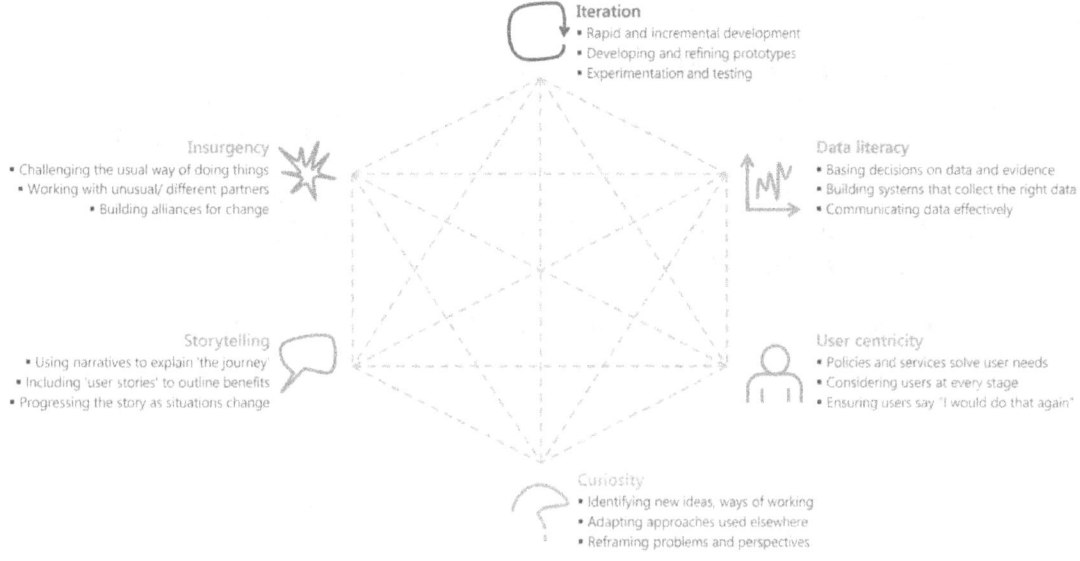

Source: (OECD, 2017[3])

Contribution from the European Commission Joint Research Centre

This work also builds on the European Commission Joint Research Centre's (JRC) longstanding experience of working at the intersection of science and policy. The JRC has developed a Framework for Skills for Evidence-informed policy-making, mapping the essential for researchers active in the science-policy interface. This report addresses the supply side of evidence, and analyses the set of collective skills needed for the research community to inform policy through evidence (European Commission, 2017[4]). The resulting professional development framework consists of eight skills clusters with each cluster addressing a specific part of the collective skillset required to increase the impact of research evidence on policy-making. It includes wider generic skills such as 'Interpersonal Skills' and 'Engaging with Citizens & Stakeholders' as well as skills specific to evidence-informed policy-making, such as 'Synthesising Research' and ' Monitoring & Evaluation'. Beyond this framework, the JRC is currently exploring how to understand and explain the drivers that influence policy decisions and political discourse as part of its Enlightenment 2.0 project identified above.

The European Commission has also developed a "Toolbox for a quality public administration" which aims to support, guide and encourage those who want to build public administrations that will foster prosperous, fair and resilient societies (European Commission, 2017[5]). It lays out principles and values of good governance, placing evidence at the heart of policy-making.

References

European Commission (2017), *Framework for Skills for Evidence-Informed Policy-Making | JRC Science Hub Communities*, JRC Science Hub, https://ec.europa.eu/jrc/communities/en/community/evidence4policy/news/framework-skills-evidence-informed-policy-making (accessed on 3 March 2019). [4]

European Commission (2017), *Quality of Public Administration - A Toolbox for Practitioners*, https://ec.europa.eu/social/main.jsp?catId=738&langId=en&pubId=8055&type=2&furtherPubs=no (accessed on 7 February 2019). [5]

OECD (2017), *CORE SKILLS FOR PUBLIC SECTOR INNOVATION*, https://www.oecd.org/media/oecdorg/satellitesites/opsi/contents/files/OECD_OPSI-core_skills_for_public_sector_innovation-201704.pdf (accessed on 24 January 2019). [3]

OECD (2017), *Policy Advisory Systems: Supporting Good Governance and Sound Public Decision Making*, OECD Public Governance Reviews, OECD Publishing, Paris, https://dx.doi.org/10.1787/9789264283664-en. [1]

OECD (2017), *Skills for a High Performing Civil Service*, OECD Public Governance Reviews, OECD Publishing, Paris, https://dx.doi.org/10.1787/9789264280724-en. [2]

3 What capacities and skills are needed for EIPM?

This chapter underlines the fact that use of evidence, depends on capability, motivation and opportunity. It presents a core skillset for evidence-informed policy-making (EIPM) at individual level, including the capacity for *understanding; obtaining; assessing; using; engaging with stakeholders;* and *applying evidence*. The chapter also outlines the need to build capacity for EIPM at the organisational level, where capacity for evidence use can be supported or limited by resources or organisational culture. It also underlines the role of broader environmental capacity where use of evidence use can be affected by the relationship with external organisations and societal attitudes towards evidence use.

Increasing the use of evidence depends on capability, motivation and opportunity

Increasing the use of evidence by policy-makers depends on behaviour change, such as using evidence and evaluation to influence policy debates, the resulting policy choices and the practical implementation of those choices (Langer, Tripney and Gough, 2016[1]). This can be conceptualised as components in an interacting system. The 'COM-B' model developed by Michie, van Stralen and West (2011[2]) posits that capability, opportunity and motivation interact in order to generate behaviour:

- *Capability* is defined as the individual's psychological and physical capacity to engage in the activity concerned. It includes having the necessary knowledge and skills.
- *Motivation* is defined as all the processes that energize and direct behaviour, not just goals and conscious decision-making. It includes habitual processes, emotional responding, as well as analytical decision-making.
- *Opportunity* is defined as all the factors that lie outside the individual that make the behaviour possible or prompt it.

Figure 3.1. The Capability Opportunity Motivation -Behaviour model

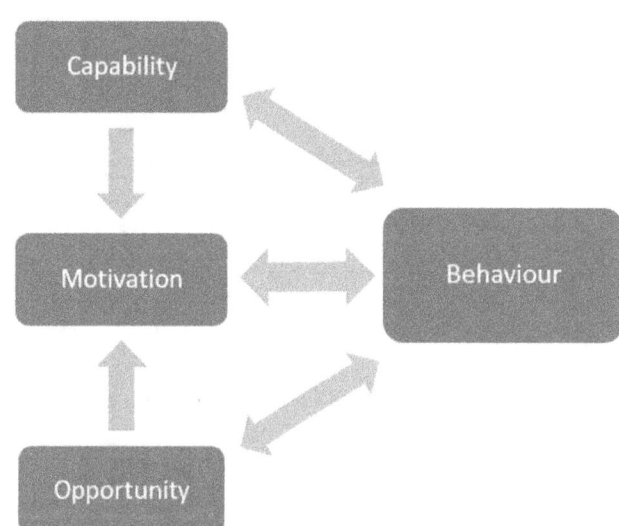

Source: (Michie, van Stralen and West, 2011[2]).

This framework has been used to characterise interventions designed to improve the design and implementation of interventions to increase the use of evidence by policy-makers (Langer, Tripney and Gough, 2016[1]). By changing capability, motivation or opportunity, separately or in combination, it can lead to creating the desired behavioural change. For example, in some cases the only barrier might be capability, in another a lack of opportunity, while in another, changes to all three might be necessary (Michie, van Stralen and West, 2011[2]). Capability to engage in EIPM includes an individual civil servant's knowledge of different types of research methods, as well as fundamental skills of statistical and data literacy and the capacity to read and understand analytical products, often in English language. Motivation to engage in EIPM can include factors such as a civil servant's belief that they have a mandate to use evidence, that the use of evidence will be rewarded and an understanding of how the use of evidence will improve the quality of policy-making and will ultimately make policies more trustworthy. The opportunity to engage in EIPM includes the strength of the connections between the policy-making and the research community and civil servant's institutional access to evidence.

Addressing capacity at multiple levels

Building capacity for EIPM necessities consideration of the changes to capability, motivation and opportunity that will lead to the desired behaviour change. Critically, building capacity for EIPM also requires consideration of multiple levels, including individuals, teams, organisations or institutions and the wider environment. This is because 'capacity' is a multidimensional concept spanning different levels from the individual, interpersonal, organisational and environmental, with each of these levels shaping behaviour (Newman, Fisher and Shaxson, 2012[3]; OECD, 2017[4]). Each of these levels is likely to require different forms of capacity building initiatives (Haynes et al., 2018[5]). Furthermore, no level operates in isolation, they interact with each other, reinforcing or weakening each other. A visual presentation of the various levels is presented in Figure 3.2, which illustrates how the capacities for the use of evidence can exist within complex and multi-layered systems.

Figure 3.2. A model for increasing the use of evidence by policy-makers at multiple levels

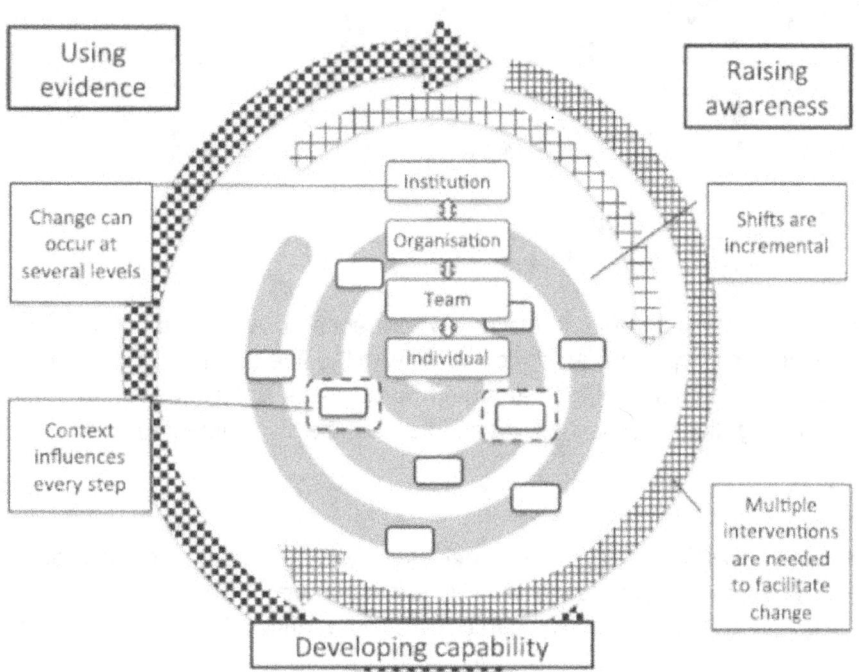

Source: Stewart, Langer and Erasmus (2018[6]).

Towards a relevant set of skills, knowledge and attitudes for individuals

Individual capacity is the combination of capability, motivation and opportunity which together affect behaviour (Newman, Fisher and Shaxson, 2012[3]). Therefore, the first major step towards building capacity for evidence-informed policy-making is to specify the skills and competencies required for effective use of evidence and evaluation by the civil service.

The mapping of the relevant skills and competencies benefitted from a close cooperation between the OECD and the Joint Research Centre of the European Commission. This included an expert workshop held at the OECD in April 2018, in collaboration with country experts. The outcome of the workshop includes the six skills presented below for Understanding, Obtaining, Interrogating and Assessing, Using and Applying, Engaging with Stakeholders and Evaluating (see Figure 3.3). Although grouped in six skills clusters for the purposes of clarity, in practice the use of these competences is interconnected and not bound to a specific policy process or action. A number of these skills are of a crosscutting character and are applied in multiple occasions, such as critical thinking, systems thinking, engaging with stakeholders. These competences also need to be viewed as a collective skill-set for the public service of tomorrow rather than a full list of skills that each public servant needs to master.

Figure 3.3. The Skillset for Evidence-informed Policy-making

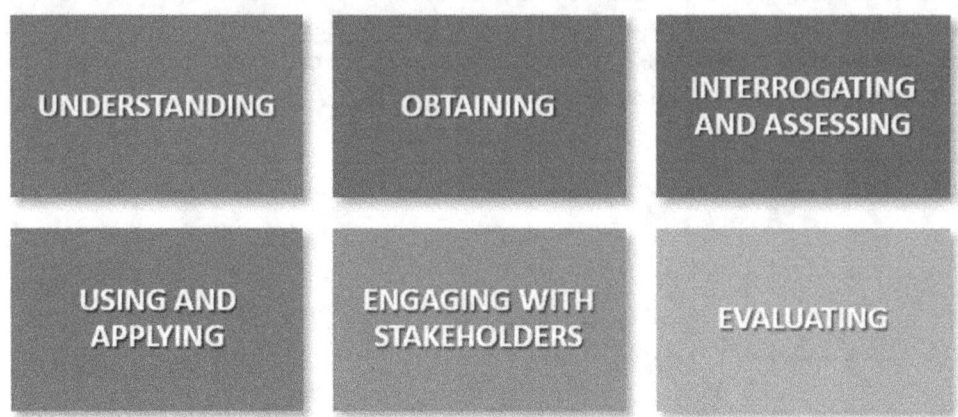

Understanding evidence-informed policy-making

Policy-makers with this skill will understand the role of evidence and its place in the policy-making cycle, as well as the challenges and opportunities, which come with the use of evidence. This will be underpinned by knowledge of different research methods and their purpose, as well as the fundamentals of statistical and data literacy (including big data, machine learning and artificial intelligence).

Obtaining evidence

Policy-makers[1] with this skill will be able to gather existing evidence in their own policy area and know who to turn to as sources of evidence synthesis. They will be able to recognise where there are evidence gaps and commission high quality evidence to fill these gaps using a range of project management techniques.

Interrogating and assessing evidence

Policy-makers with this skill will make use of a set of holistic, systemic and critical thinking tools. They will be able to assess the provenance, reliability and appropriateness of evidence. They will have an ability to interrogate evidence by critically assessing its quality and context, using a range of techniques to challenge assumptions and biases.

Using and applying evidence in the policy-making

Policy-makers with this skill will understand their own policy context and recognise possible uses of evidence in the policy cycle. They will be proficient in knowledge management and understand the role of innovation, with an ability to assess and manage risks and challenges. They will be familiar with and know when to use innovative techniques like behavioural insights, design thinking, policy labs and foresight to support policy design and implementation.

Engaging with stakeholders in evidence-informed policy-making

Policy-makers with this skill will have strong engagement and communication skills, including the ability to create effective evidence-based messages for different types of audiences and to engage and inspire a variety of stakeholders. They will be able to manage and facilitate evidence-informed debate with policy-makers and citizens and maintain collaboration with the evidence community. They will have a good grasp of co-creation, co-production and participatory methodologies.

Evaluating the success of evidence-informed policy-making

Policy-makers with this skill will understand different evaluation approaches and tools, and know-how to use comparative examples to inform EIPM. They will understand that evaluation should be built in the policy cycle and should serve to inform and improve EIPM. They will know and use qualitative and quantitative indicators of successful evidence use.

Building capacity for EIPM uptake at the organisational level

Organisational capacity encompasses factors, which can either support or impede the use of evidence within organisations. This can include tangible factors such as well-maintained computer facilities, adequately resourced libraries and robust knowledge management processes. The dissemination and translation of the evidence cannot take place if such resources are not available or cannot be accessed in time.

Developing an evidence strategy can be an important way of ensuring institutional memory, which prevents organizational knowledge from vanishing altogether with the churn of staff. This requires a proper strategy for knowledge management within the civil service. Evidence strategies should set the strategic direction for how evidence will be generated and used, the learning and development needed, and consideration of what capacity building might need the recruitment or contracting of certain specialist skills (such as data science) The long-term institutionalisation of EIPM can be facilitated by the machinery of government, such as a strategy unit or another entity at the centre of government with a clear responsibility and mandate over EIPM.

Organisational capacity also includes less tangible factors such as the political context and organisational culture, which can also impact the demand for evidence (Newman, Fisher and Shaxson, 2012[3]). 'Culture' refers to the norms, values, and basic assumptions of a given organization (Damschroder et al., 2009[7]). One explanation for why so many change initiatives fail is that they fail to tackle these less tangible elements of an organisation's capacity. Organisational capacity may also entail the capacity to access a full range of evidence and evaluation, overcoming some structural biases. For example, the contribution of behavioural sciences and social sciences can also be very important in very specific or technical fields, while ministries competent in those areas may tend to rely primarily on very technical or engineering capacity, overlooking the need for broader and more holistic approaches.

An organisation's technical capacity, climate and culture collectively affect employee performance, including the adoption of innovative and evidence-based practices (Makkar et al., 2015[8]; Oliver et al., 2014[9]). Furthermore, policy-makers' use of evidence can be improved if their organisations have a receptive attitude and culture towards evidence and use and invest in resources that support research use. These organisational factors can be understood with reference to the COM-B framework, in that organisational factors provide the incentives, which motivate the individual to use evidence (or not). For example, in a civil service, which explicitly includes the use of evidence in its competency framework, this may provide an incentive, which motivates civil servants to use evidence in their policy development. Organisational factors also enhance or constrain opportunities for individuals to use evidence. For example, a civil service, which has established systems for civil servants to be able to access research (such of research portals and journal access) and to come into contact with members of the research community, has increased opportunities for civil servants to use evidence compared to a civil service in which this activities are absent or difficult to access.

The role of wider environmental capacity

The wider environment beyond organisational boundaries also affects the demand for evidence. In the context of national governments, the wider capacity can refer to the extent to which ministries and departments are networked with other external organisations who can support evidence use, as organisations that support and promote external boundary-spanning roles of their employees are more likely to implement innovative practices quickly (Damschroder et al., 2009[7]) (Greenhalgh et al., 2004[10]).

Wider capacity is also related to government strategies to spread interventions, including policies and regulations, and also recommendations and guidelines. Decisions about how to gather, analyse and interpret evidence will also be shaped by the internal dynamics of individual government departments, as well as the wider bureaucratic and political pressures (Shaxson, 2019[11]). This includes civil service reform programmes, organisational cultures and internal structures and processes that impact upon how individuals and teams work with each other.

Cultural and attitudinal factors in the wider society also affect the extent to which evidence gets used in policy-making. Societal attitudes towards policy-making, and what and who should contribute to it, can also impact the use of evidence in policy-making (Newman, Fisher and Shaxson, 2012[3]). This is also connected to ideas about political accountability, the extent to which elected officials are held accountable by state or civil society organisations, including the media, for the quality of their policy-making (Newman, Fisher and Shaxson, 2012[3]). The extent to which there is a culture of inquiry and how this is developed through institutions such as higher education also determines the extent to which evidence is seen to be an important input to the policy process (Newman, Fisher and Shaxson, 2012[3]).

References

Damschroder, L. et al. (2009), "Fostering implementation of health services research findings into practice: a consolidated framework for advancing implementation science", *Implementation Science*, Vol. 4/1, p. 50, http://dx.doi.org/10.1186/1748-5908-4-50.	[7]
Greenhalgh, T. et al. (2004), "Diffusion of Innovations in Service Organizations: Systematic Review and Recommendations", *The Milbank Quarterly*, Vol. 82/4, pp. 581-629, http://dx.doi.org/10.1111/j.0887-378X.2004.00325.x.	[10]
Haynes, A. et al. (2018), "What can we learn from interventions that aim to increase policy-makers' capacity to use research? A realist scoping review", *Health Research Policy and Systems*, Vol. 16/1, p. 31, http://dx.doi.org/10.1186/s12961-018-0277-1.	[5]
Langer, L., J. Tripney and D. Gough (2016), *The science of using science: researching the use of Research evidence in decision-making.*.	[1]
Makkar, S. et al. (2015), "The development of ORACLe: a measure of an organisation's capacity to engage in evidence-informed health policy", *Health Research Policy and Systems*, Vol. 14/1, p. 4, http://dx.doi.org/10.1186/s12961-015-0069-9.	[8]

Michie, S., M. van Stralen and R. West (2011), "The behaviour change wheel: A new method for characterising and designing behaviour change interventions", *Implementation Science*, Vol. 6/1, p. 42, http://dx.doi.org/10.1186/1748-5908-6-42. [2]

Newman, K., C. Fisher and L. Shaxson (2012), "Stimulating Demand for Research Evidence: What Role for Capacity-building?", *IDS Bulletin*, Vol. 43/5, pp. 17-24, http://dx.doi.org/10.1111/j.1759-5436.2012.00358.x. [3]

OECD (2017), *Skills for a High Performing Civil Service*, OECD Public Governance Reviews, OECD Publishing, Paris, https://dx.doi.org/10.1787/9789264280724-en. [4]

Oliver, K. et al. (2014), "A systematic review of barriers to and facilitators of the use of evidence by policymakers", *BMC Health Services Research*, Vol. 14/1, http://dx.doi.org/10.1186/1472-6963-14-2. [9]

Shaxson, L. (2019), "Uncovering the practices of evidence-informed policy-making", *Public Money & Management*, Vol. 39/1, pp. 46-55, http://dx.doi.org/10.1080/09540962.2019.1537705. [11]

Stewart, R., L. Langer and Y. Erasmus (2018), "An integrated model for increasing the use of evidence by decision-makers for improved development", *Development Southern Africa*, pp. 1-16, http://dx.doi.org/10.1080/0376835X.2018.1543579. [6]

Note

[1] Although this report recognises the importance of elected officials as consumers of evidence, 'Policy-makers' refers primarily to senior members of the civil service responsible for the substantive tasks of policy design and implementation.

4 What interventions, strategies and tools can strengthen capacity for EIPM?

This chapter discusses the barriers and facilitators that may affect the use of evidence in policy-making, and offers a mapping of existing initiatives that seek to strengthen the EIPM skill set, in terms of understanding, obtaining, interrogating and assessing, using and applying, engaging and evaluating. It also discusses diagnostic tools to evaluate organisational capacities for EIPM and initiatives to build organisational capacities for EIPM.

The policy-making process is complex with many barriers and facilitators that affect the use of evidence. This chapter will map some of the barriers and facilitators to the use of evidence and will provide tools and descriptions of initiatives that address many of the barriers. The tools described below assist in improving each of the six core skills for policy-makers described in chapter 3. These tools work at both at an individual and organisational level to increase the use of evidence in the policy-making process.

Identifying barriers and facilitators

Multiple dimensions of capacity affect the use of evidence in policy-making. Therefore, to build successful strategies, it is necessary to understand what are the barriers and facilitators to evidence-informed policy-making. Oliver et al. (2014[1]) in a systematic review (with 145 studies carried out it over 59 countries), found that timely access to high quality and relevant research, collaborations with policy-makers and relationship and skill building with policy-makers were reported to be the most important factors in influencing the use of evidence. Their research identified five categories, which encompass factors that can work as either facilitators or barriers depending on how they are managed (see Figure 4.1). The role of the various barriers and facilitators to evidence-informed policy-making will vary between contexts. The list below may not be exhaustive. The way in which specific barriers and facilitators operate, and how they interact with each other, will be context-specific.

Figure 4.1. Barriers and Facilitators to EIPM

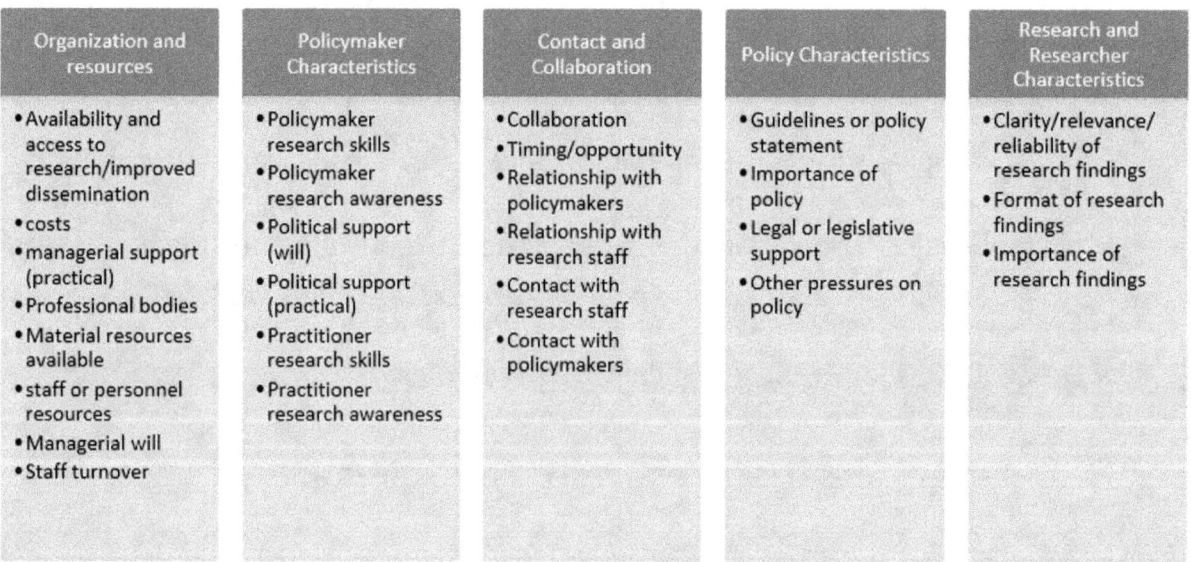

Source: (Oliver et al., 2014[1]).

Therefore, implementing any strategy and interventions to strengthen capacity for use of evidence, will require a first gap analysis and scan of the existing barriers and facilitators that prevail in a given national context.

How can governments identify and select appropriate strategies?

Given the complexity of policy-making and the myriad of barriers that stand in the way of using evidence in policy-making, a range of interventions, strategies and tools are necessary. There is no one strategy that can be identified as superior to others in building the capacity of policy-makers to use evidence, rather a combination of strategies that are responsive to the dynamic contextual conditions of each jurisdiction is likely to be most effective in promoting sustainable change.

Although most capacity building initiatives are multifaceted, involving more than one strategy and aiming at more than one outcome, it is nevertheless possible to draw broad distinctions between different types of initiatives and to map these onto the skills framework presented in the previous chapter, which was jointly designed, by the OECD and the JRC. A summary of this mapping is presented in Figure 4.2[1]. A more detailed mapping of interventions, strategies and tools onto the skills framework for EIPM in presented in Annex A.

There is great potential for the tools listed in this chapter to be used more widely to provide a formal needs analysis of current capacity for EIPM, which then facilitates consultative approaches to choosing a range of interventions that are tailored to the local needs and context. For example, a recent review of interventions found that whilst many interventions were described as 'tailored' only a minority had actually used formal needs analysis to shape the intervention to meet local needs (Haynes et al., 2018[2]).

Beyond these specific initiatives, it is also critical to understand how to embed these approaches within organisational structures and systems. This can be done through systemic or organisational approaches, which are analysed in the following chapter.

Figure 4.2. Mapping existing initiatives against the OECD/JRC skills framework

Understanding	Obtaining	Interrogating and Assessing	Using and Applying	Engaging	Evaluating
•Diagnostic Tools of indvidual capacity e.g. Australia's Staff Assessment of enGagement with Evidence •Senior Civil Service programmes e.g. Finland's Public Sector Leadership training	•Access to online databases e.g. Campbell Collaboration •Disseminating tailored syntheses of evidence e.g. Argentina's Policy Research briefs and Clearinghouses in the US •Commissioning research and reviews e.g. UK's Policy Reviews Facility • Seminars to present research findings e.g. The Joint Research Centre's lunchtime lecture series	•Intensive skills training programmes e.g. INGSA's capacity building initatives. •Knowledge brokers (organisations) e.g. Poland's - Centre for Evaluation and Analysis of Public Policies.	•Intensive skills training programmes e.g. OECD/Mexico's Capacity Building for RIA •Knowledge brokers (individuals) e.g. New Zealand's Chief Science Advisor •Mentoring e.g. South Africa's mentoring programme for policy makers	•One-off or periodic interactive forums e.g. Joint Research Centre's Evidence and policy summer school' • Platforms for ongoing interactivity e.g. The global Preventing Violence Across the Lifespan Network •Partnership projects e.g. the Netherlands Academic Collaborative Centres and the US' National Poverty Research Center	•Diagnostic tools of organisational capacity for evidence use e.g. Canada's Evidence Literacy diagnostic tool

Diagnostic tools to promote understanding of evidence

A key first step in any capacity building programme is to promote *understanding*. This includes understanding if there is a desire for change and finding out which of the core processes of policy-making support or hinder an evidence-informed approach. Without such an understanding, government agencies risk investing in strategies that are poorly matched to their needs and therefore wasting opportunities to enhance their use of evidence. These tools attempt to understand the existing capability, motivation and opportunity to use evidence within the system.

There is great potential for these tools to be used more widely to provide a formal needs analysis of current capacity for EIPM, which then facilitates consultative approaches to choosing an approach range of interventions that are tailored to the local needs and context. For example, a recent review of interventions found that whilst many interventions were described as 'tailored' only a minority had actually used formal needs analysis to shape the intervention to meet local needs (Haynes et al., 2018[2]).

Australia has developed a number of tools to measure policy-makers' capacity to engage with and use research. The Seeking, Engaging with and Evaluating Research (SEER) is a tool to measure individual policy-maker's capacity to engage with and use research (Brennan et al., 2017[3]). SEER is envisaged as a practical tool that can help policy agencies that want to assess and develop their capacity for using research, as well as a tool to evaluate the success of initiatives designed to improve evidence use in policy-making.

SEER uses a questionnaire consisting of 50 questions and is broken into three categories of assessment to identify areas for improvement in the use of research. The first category, *capacity,* measures whether an individual has the motivation and capability to engage with research and researchers. *Research Engagement Actions* measures the systematic process for engaging with research, including actions that are likely to be precursors to the use of research. *Research Use* measures the extent and way in which research is used to inform the different stages of policy or programme development. Policy agencies can use this tool by having their policy-makers fill out the questionnaire. Policy agencies will then be able to determine which areas to focus on to improve the use of evidence by policy-makers. For more details on each category see Figure 4.3.

Figure 4.3. Seeking, Engaging with and Evaluating Research (SEER)

Tool for policy-makers to assess and develop their capacity to use research.

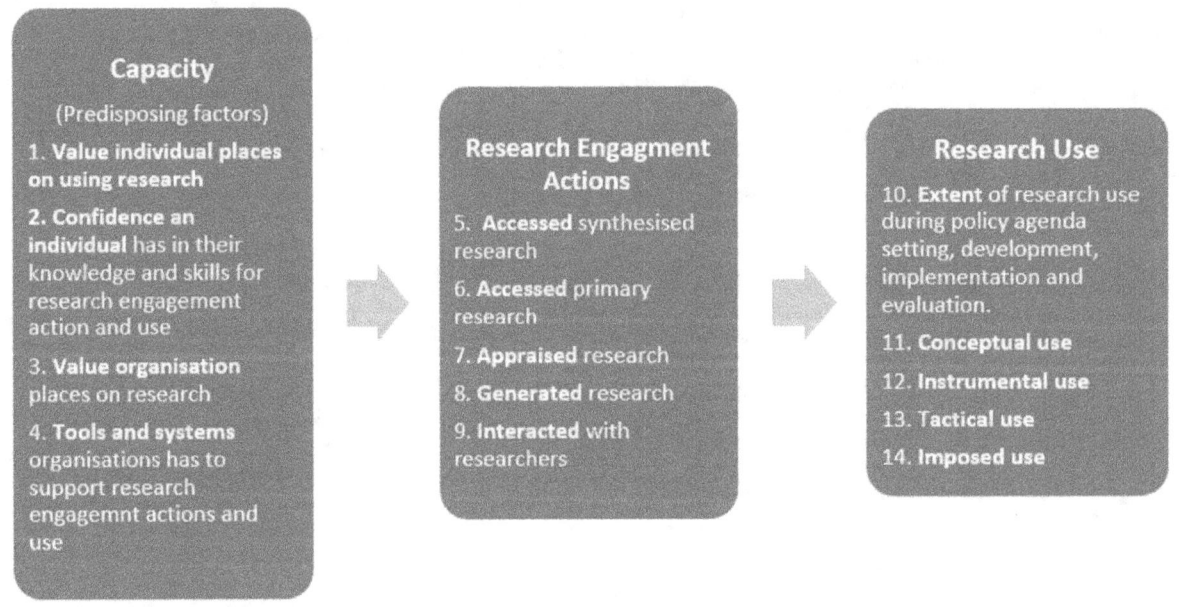

Source: (Brennan et al., 2017[3]).

The Staff Assessment of engagement with Evidence (SAGE) is a further tool that has been developed in Australia and aims to provide a thorough evaluation of current levels of research engagement and use; and it also works to inform interventions to improve research capacity and evaluate their success (R. Makkar et al., 2016[4]; Makkar et al., 2017[5]). SAGE combines an interview and document analysis to concretely assess how policy-makers engaged with research, how research was used and what barriers impacted the use of research in relation to a specific policy product. Following promising preliminary testing of the tool's reliability and validity (Makkar et al., 2017[5]) it would be possible to train agency staff to use SAGE to assess research use within their agencies. This would help to inform the type of tools, systems and structures agencies could invest in to improve how staff use evidence and also to evaluate the effectiveness of these tools, systems and structures.

Initiatives to increase policy-makers' ability to obtain evidence

Policy-makers cannot use research evidence if they do not know about it (Haynes et al., 2018[2]). Therefore, strategies that increase access to clearly presented research findings is one promising approach to increase research use. These strategies include: providing access to research through online databases; disseminating tailored syntheses of research evidence; commissioning research and reviews; seminars to present research findings; and access to knowledge brokers. Mapping these interventions onto the OECD/JRC framework, they all share a core focus of improving policy-makers ability to *obtain* evidence. In terms of the behaviour change model, these interventions are generally trying to increase opportunities for policy-makers to use evidence.

Evaluations of such initiatives show that, in general, tailored and contextualised syntheses, seminars and advice from knowledge brokers and researchers seem to be the most promising means of improving access to research. Overall, research suggests that in isolation, improved access alone does not significantly improve evidence-informed policy-making (Haynes et al., 2018[2]; Langer, Tripney and Gough, 2016[6]; Dobbins et al., 2009[7]). In contrast, interventions facilitating access have been found to be effective when the intervention simultaneously tries to enhance policy-makers' opportunity and motivation to use evidence (Langer, Tripney and Gough, 2016[6]; Haynes et al., 2018[2]).

Access to research through online databases

Providing policy-makers with access to research articles or syntheses via an online database aims to maximise access to specific types of research and increase policy-makers' confidence in accessing and using such content.

The Campbell Collaboration and The Cochrane Library, established 20 years ago, aim to improve the quality of healthcare policy-making. Cochrane is a global independent network of researchers, professionals, patients, carers and people interested in health. The Cochrane Library contains systematic reviews of medical and healthcare interventions. The Campbell Collaboration promotes positive social and economic change through the production and use of systematic reviews and other evidence synthesis for evidence-informed policy and practice. The Campbell Library covers the following areas: crime and justice, disability, education, international development, knowledge translation and implementation, nutrition and social welfare.

Disseminating tailored syntheses of evidence

One approach to increasing policy-makers' motivation to use evidence is to tailor it to their needs. In general, the increased ease of access and use of evidence resulting when evidence was synthesised, tailored for specific users and sent directly to them, facilitated uptake of evidence use by policy-makers (Haynes et al., 2018[2]). An example of this are contextualised and individualised evidence briefs (Langer, Tripney and Gough, 2016[6]; Haynes et al., 2018[2]).

The WHO launched a programme to support evidence-informed policy-making in a number of low- and middle-income countries (Shroff et al., 2015[8]). In Argentina, the programme focused on the production of policy briefs on health research and holding policy dialogues. OECD's work on knowledge brokering institutions, also shows that policy briefs are common tools for trying to disseminate research to policy-makers (OECD, 2018[9]). For example, the UK What Works Centre, including Education Endowment Foundation, the Early Intervention and the What Works Centre for Local Economic Growth produce a range of policy briefs to disseminate key messages to its target audience.

Tailored research products are perceived as credible, useful and likely to impact decision-making and seem to add value over and above simply providing access to the primary research.

While many organisations do produce policy briefs to disseminate their research, practices are also influenced by social media. Policy briefs can also be replaced by "information nuggets", and parts of storytelling that can be disseminated through social media accounts, to spread the main messages of key policy and evaluation reports. While these may limit the substantive content of what is actually disseminated, it is also believed to be a way to increase the impact in a wider sense. If citizens are aware of the results and wary of the implications, it will also build pressure on the policy-makers to pay attention to the results and ensure that they feed into policy-making.

Commissioning research and reviews

Policy-makers commissioning research and reviews of research is hypothesised to increase their engagement with and control of the research which in turn would increase the relevance and applicability of the research to policy-making (Haynes et al., 2018[2]).

In Australia, the 'Evidence Check' programme was developed to assist Australian policy-makers in commissioning high-quality reviews of research to inform policy decisions. The programme involved an iterative process of knowledge brokering in order to formulate and refine the scope of and questions addressed by the review (Campbell et al., 2011[10]). In the UK, the Department of Health and Social Care developed a 'Policy Reviews Facility' to support national policy development and implementation which has existed in some form since 1995 (EPPI Centre, 2016[11]). Policy teams, government analysts and academic experts from three universities (University College London, University of York and London School and Hygiene and Tropical Medicine) work closely together to determine the focus of systematic review products to best meet the needs of policy work. In the US, the OMB has developed grant review and support structures to assess the quality of evidence being commissioned.

Commissioned research facilitated by a knowledge broker has been found to be useful and accurate by the policy-makers who commissioned them. They were mostly used in indirect ways, such as informing policy deliberations and providing background information (Haynes et al., 2018[2]). Feedback from policy-makers and researchers on the Evidence Check suggested that the use of knowledge brokers enhanced the value of reviews commissioned (Campbell et al., 2011[10]).

Seminars to present research findings

Seminars can provide policy relevant accessible content, the success of which seems to be enhanced by the credibility and communication skills of the presenter. It is also hypothesized that such meetings can be a useful way of bringing policy-makers and researchers together, breaking the ice which could lead to further interactions.

The Joint Research Centre at the European Commission has held a lunchtime science lecture series for a number of years. The seminars feature JRC scientists and researchers, as well as external guest speakers. The seminars are web streamed and announced carousel on the JRC's homepage and twitter account (EU Science Hub, 2019[12]).

Seminars are generally well received by attendees and preferred to reading reports. However, results are less positive concerning the ability of seminars in isolation to lead to behaviour change and impact on policy-making (Haynes et al., 2018[2]; Langer, Tripney and Gough, 2016[6]).

Access to knowledge brokers

Knowledge brokers can help to facilitate policy-makers' access to research evidence by helping them to navigate research material that may be unfamiliar. They can also help to articulate policy-maker's needs, constraints and expectations, translating them for researchers who may be unfamiliar with the policy process. Factors that facilitate the success of knowledge brokers include their interpersonal skills, ability to provide individualised support and perceived neutrality (Haynes et al., 2018[2]).

Knowledge brokers can include individual professionals and dedicated organisations. Government Chief Science Advisors are one example of individual knowledge brokers present in some countries. In terms of institutions, some are specifically connected to knowledge producers, such as brokering units within academic institutions (Kauffeld-Monz and Fritsch, 2013[13]). Examples of such organizations are the Centre for Evaluation and Analysis of Public Policies in Poland and the Top Institute of Evidence-Based Education Research in the Netherlands. Other approaches locate the knowledge broker function closer the decision makers, either in a body at arm's length from government or within a relevant agency itself. Examples of this approach include activities carried out by the Australian Institute for Family Studies (AIFS) and the Research and Evaluation Unit Department of Children and Youth Affair in Ireland. In France, many of these knowledge brokerage functions are integrated within the ministries, with the analytical units in the Ministries of Labor (DARES), Social Affairs (DREES), or the Environment (DEEE), providing strategic advice and access to evidence, integrating the knowledge broker functions within the day-to-day activities of the ministries.

Evaluations of knowledge brokering activities have found that it is regarded as helpful and preferable to training and other tools, although not all studies have found an added value of knowledge brokering compared to other activities. Other studies have shown that working with a knowledge broker can increase policy-makers' knowledge and skills in finding, appraising and using evidence, leading to increased engagement in evidence based policy-making (Haynes et al., 2018[2]).

Improving policy-makers' capacity to interrogate, assess, use and apply evidence

Stimulating demand for research requires significant behaviour change from individuals working in policy-making, and these changes are unlikely to be achieved in a single training workshop, especially if the workshop is delivered in a didactic manner (Newman, Fisher and Shaxson, 2012[14]). Nevertheless, this does not mean that there is no role for training initiatives in building capacity for EIPM. Although there are differences between these in the goals of different initiatives, many are focused specifically on improving individual capability to use research.

Existing country practice reveals a wide range and approaches towards skills development interventions. This includes both training designed to encourage managers such as the Senior Civil Service to become champions of research use (as well as more intensive skills training programmes for policy professionals. Senior Civil Service leadership training is primarily aimed at increasing managers' *understanding* of EIPM, enabling them to become champions for evidence use. Intensive skills training programmes vary in content and format but can be focused on *interrogating and assessing* evidence and also on *using and applying* it in policy-making.

Factors that lead to successful training include having participant-driven learning, active input and a strengths-based approach that motivates and assures policy-makers of their abilities. It is also critical that there is strong leadership support for attendance at such training, which is indicative of the wider organisational commitment to the use of research. Shorter more intensive programmes have been associated with increased retention. Some studies have also found that training can be undermined by high staff turnover and conflicting work pressures. There can also be a trade-off between the intensity of training and policy-makers ability to attend, especially with senior policy-makers who have a critical role to play in championing change (Haynes et al., 2018[2]).

OECD's work on how to engage public employees for a high performing civil service highlights the importance of learning and training in a modern civil service, to enable civil servants to continually update their skills and capacity to innovate (OECD, 2016[15]). There is a strong justification for investment in learning and training and there is also a strong call from employers and employees for the need to invest in skill and competency development. Therefore, rigorous evaluation of initiatives is critical in order to invest in the most cost-efficient interventions, without comprising their effectiveness.

Senior civil service leadership training to build an understanding of EIPM

Training managers, such as the Senior Civil Service (SCS) on research evidence use can create a shift in work culture and increase the use of evidence within their team. Through training, managers can learn to foster an environment that enables and promotes the use of evidence in policy-making.

In Canada, the Executive Training in Research Application (EXTRA) programme provides support and development for leaders in using research. The programme is targeted at leaders in the healthcare field. The programme's objectives are that after the completion of the training, participants will be able to use evidence in their policy-making and will be able to train their co-workers and bring about organizational change. Finland also has developed public sector leadership training, which is described in Box 4.1.

Box 4.1. Public Sector Leadership training in Finland

SITRA, the Finnish Innovation Fund, is an independent public foundation, which operates directly under the supervision of the Finnish Parliament.

Since 2017, SITRA has organised Public Sector Leadership training, to strengthen the ability of public-sector leaders to handle challenges and supports the public sector in the reform of its social role. In order to meet the needs of senior management of ministries and agencies, a training programme that includes six modules was developed, covering the following topics:

1. global phenomena and the public sector's ability to renew;
2. new operating models for complex phenomena;
3. alternative systematic approaches from around the world (international study trip)
4. from public administration to service;
5. leading people and renewing the leadership culture;
6. putting new practices and lessons learned from experiments into practice.

The training groups are compiled cross-governmentally so that each course includes representatives from different ministries and agencies. In addition to expert presentations, the training includes workshops, practical interim assignments that support learning, peer sparring and practice experiments related to the current challenges of administration and enabling leadership.

Source: Adapted from SITRA (2017[16]).

The Portuguese government also recognises the importance of the Senior Civil Service's role in maintaining a focus on performance and results. On an annual basis, all public service organisations inform the National Institute of Public Administration of employees' training needs, which then feeds into the development of an annual training programme (OECD, 2016[17]). Alongside this, the government has identified new competencies for the public management of complex policy challenges. This includes a focus on performance and results, innovation, communication as well as core management and leadership skills.

In Mexico, academic institutions and non-governmental organisations have been instrumental in promoting a culture of evidence-informed policy-making by developing the next generation of the senior civil service as champions of an evidence-informed approach. As a specific example, IREFAM, a private institution offering graduate studies to mental health professionals in the state of Chihuahua, altered the content of its masters and doctoral programmes in collaboration with the University of Texas at Austin, to include material on evidence-based prevention interventions with a specific focus on cultural adaptation. Since 2007, over 500 master's students have been trained in these approaches, with many now occupying leadership positions in state government thus enabling them to actively promote the implementation of evidence-based prevention interventions (Parra-Cardona et al., 2018[18]).

National Schools of Government also play an important role in civil service skills and knowledge development. According to OECD research, schools are principally involved in activities that are related to training and professional development activities, such as organising conferences, integrity and value training, and management and leadership development. Examples of the missions and mandates of three schools can be found in Box 4.2.

> **Box 4.2. National schools of government: Missions and Mandates**
>
> **Colombia's Superior School of Public Administration**
>
> - To educate citizens in the knowledge, values and skills that are used in the public administrative field for the development of society and the State and for the enhancement of management capacity of entities and organisations that provide public service, at the different levels of higher education, education for work and human development, research and technical assistance in regional, national and global contexts.
>
> **Latvian School of Public Administration (LSPA)**
>
> - The LSPA provides a high-quality training and consultation service to meet the current and future needs of public administration and municipalities. The training and services developed by the LSPA help further to ensure a high quality of public service in Latvia. The LSPA is the largest training centre for civil servants and public administration employees in Latvia. The LSPA develops open and tailor-made training for both the public and private sectors, and oversees the certification of internal audit specialists in public service.
>
> **Spain's National Institute of Public Administration (INAP)**
>
> - While the main tasks of the INAP have traditionally been training and improvement of the civil service, nowadays it performs a wide array of activities that may be classified in the following areas: 1) recruitment into the civil service; 2) training and professional improvement of public employees; 3) research and publishing and 4) international relations. In addition, the Institute carries out a wide variety of educational and academic activities, intergovernmental co-operation and the analysis of public policies through conferences, meetings and seminars.
>
> Source: OECD (2017[19]).

Intensive skills training programmes to interrogate and assess evidence

Training programmes geared towards policy-makers can provide them with the necessary skills to increase the use of evidence in their work. Training programmes can be very effective when they are learner-centred and participatory, ideally embedded within long-term strategies for professional development (Newman, Fisher and Shaxson, 2012[14]).

Creating learner-focused programmes can include tailoring content to individual needs, informal information exchange and practice opportunities. Through trainings, policy-makers not only learn a new skill but often also have increased motivation to use evidence and many become research champions and train or mentor others (Haynes et al., 2018[2]).

In the UK, the Alliance for Useful Evidence has an Evidence Masterclass where policy-makers can learn about how to use evidence in their policy work and can practice their new skills through simulations. Through this programme, policy-makers are able to build their confidence in compiling, assimilating, distilling, interpreting and presenting evidence. Participants learn how to find research that is relevant to their policy question and develop their ability to assess of quality and trustworthiness of research. In Sweden, the Swedish Agency for Health Technology Assessment and Assessment of Social Services also has a training programme for evidence use in policy-making.

Mexico has also implemented capacity-building initiatives towards Regulatory Impact Assessment. Regulatory Impact Analysis (RIA) is a systemic approach to critically assessing the positive and negative effects of proposed and existing regulations and non-regulatory alternatives. Conducting RIA can underpin the capacity of governments to ensure that regulations are efficient and effective. For example, training seminars were held by Mexico's Ministry of the Economy, for Federal and Provincial officials on how to draft and implement Regulatory Impact Assessments (RIA). The learning programme provided a step-by-step methodology on how to produce and analyse impact assessments in practice using guidance, case studies and advice from peer government officials, experts and the OECD. (Adapted from OECD (2012[20]).

Poland is another country that has implemented capacity-building initiatives geared towards RIA in the form of an Academy for Regulatory Impact Assessment initiated by the Chancellery of the Prime Minister. The basic aim of the academy is to develop competencies and skills of the civil servants responsible for the preparation of legal acts. As part of the project, participants are offered: As part of the project, participants are offered: 1) post-graduate studies in the field of regulatory impact assessment and public consultations 2) long-term specialist trainings on public consultations 3) continuous training in the field of the application of analytical techniques as part of the impact assessment (regulatory impact assessments and public consultations).

Training programs are also a key function for advisory bodies and international networks to improve the science to policy interface and contribute to evidence-informed policy-making. For instance, The International Network for Government Science Advice (INGSA) works as a collaborative platform for policy exchange, capacity building and research across diverse global science advisory organisations and national systems (See Box 4.3).

Box 4.3. The International Network for Government Science Advice – Capacity Building Initiatives

Capacity building workshops have been held across the world, including in Belgium, Brazil, Canada, Denmark, Germany, Norway and Slovakia. Although the content and format can vary, they are typically delivered in collaboration with local partners and other organisations working at the science policy interface.

- In Canada, the workshop explored topics surrounding the concept of 'diversity' in science advice, including: the multiple levels of governance in federal systems; linguistic and cultural diversity and indigenous knowledge systems; the input from academies and other established organisations; the impact of diverse industrial sectors, among others.
- In Norway, the seminar discussed issues of governmental science and how to share best practices and perspectives on science advice to government.

Source: adapted from Wilsdon, Saner and Gluckman (2018[21]) and INGSA (2019[22]).

The European Commission Joint Research Centre's (JRC) launched in 2018 a pilot initiative called "Science meets Parliaments/Science meets Regions", involving the organisation of events in 22 member states, bringing together scientists, policy-makers as well as businesses and civil society organisations in order to promote evidence-informed policies on specific topics of local concern. The project involves targeted studies on these topics commissioned by the authorities involved, and a series of training courses on EIPM skills for policy-makers bringing together policy-makers and suppliers of evidence". See Box 4.4.

> **Box 4.4. Science meets Parliaments/Science meets Regions**
>
> This initiative includes the organisation of events at national/regional/local level; studies in support of the events; and trainings for policy-makers. Particularly, the trainings for policy-makers comprise a series of three-two days training courses for national/regional/local policy-makers, where they are taught skills to obtain, assess and use evidence, including newer tools like big data and machine learning, and how to guide evidence through the "policy machinery" without having it diluted in the process.
>
> This initiative provides a platform for scientists, businesses, government and civil society stakeholders to meet and discuss policy challenges, informed by scientific evidence while taking into account the role of citizens as end users, and the co-production dimension of citizen engagement.
>
> Source: Adapted from the European Commission's science and knowledge service (2019[23]).

Evaluations suggest that training workshops can be a useful starting point for developing individual capacity, so long as they are appropriately tailored and allow active input from participants (Haynes et al., 2018[2]). Whilst workshops are generally well received by participants and lead to self-reported increases in knowledge skills and confidence, in isolation they are unlikely to lead to long term change in practice (Taylor et al., 2004[24]; Rushmer, Hunter and Steven, 2014[25]; Haynes et al., 2018[2]).

A recent systematic review presents conclusions on the effectiveness of interventions to build skills for EIPM. The systematic review covers seven interventions in which skill development was the sole mechanism used to improve evidence use and a further fifteen multi-mechanism interventions in which skills development was one component. The following conclusions were reached regarding the impact of the skill development interventions (Langer, Tripney and Gough, 2016[6]):

- Skills development interventions were found to be **effective** in increasing evidence use if both capacity and motivation to use evidence improved.
- Skill development interventions **built capacity** in reliable ways, especially if embedded in an educational programme focused on teaching **critical appraisal skills**.
- Skill development interventions **increase motivation** to use evidence even without explicitly targeting it.
- Skill development was found **not to be effective in multi-mechanism interventions** if the educational component is diluted and only passively affected in the combined programme.
- Skill development was found to be effective in combination with interventions to embed evidence-informed policy-making skills into organisational processes, resulting in increased motivation and opportunity to use evidence.

Mentoring initiatives to build policy-makers' capacity to use evidence

Mentoring is another approach, which can be used to support individual capacity building. Mentoring is hypothesised to work by giving personalised guidance in relation to 'real-world' application of knowledge (Haynes et al., 2018[2]; Newman, Fisher and Shaxson, 2012[14]). The success of mentoring is facilitated by a number of factors. This includes ensuring it is project and person specific and enabling the policy-makers to develop tangible skills they can directly apply to their work. The credibility of mentors is also an important factor, which can be engendered by applied expertise and strong interpersonal skills. It is also important that participants in the mentoring process are accountable for striving to integrate new skills and by being given the opportunity to demonstrate competence such through presenting their work or by having it assessed (Haynes et al., 2018[2]).

Evaluations that have used mentoring as a component have found a number of effects both in terms of process and outcomes. A review of studies found that in general evaluations find that mentoring leads to self-reported increases in skills and confidence, and participants tend to apply the skills they have learnt in practice. Mentoring can also lead to improved relationships with researchers and a strengthened culture of continuous learning. There is also evidence that mentoring may provide the greatest support to staff who are less integrated into the workforce, such as new employees who may lack confidence in using research skills (Haynes et al., 2018[2]).

> **Box 4.5. South Africa's mentoring programme**
>
> South Africa has a longstanding history of initiatives to improve the demand side for evidence use in policy-making through innovation and the institutionalisation of evidence use.
>
> To further improve the use of evidence in policy-making, workshops and a mentorship programme was implemented throughout the government. The programme was created to address the disconnect between the widespread support for EIPM in principle and its practical application.
>
> Workshops and mentorships were targeted towards the needs of the individuals participating in the programmes. The programmes recognized that individuals participating came with a wide range of starting points: some had very little awareness of evidence-informed policy-making and came to learn more, whilst others were already aware and skilled and came to explore opportunities to send colleagues along, and/or gain mentorship support.
>
> The workshops and group mentoring were geared towards laying the foundation for individuals to acquire evidence-informed policy-making skills. The group orientation created an environment in which there was greater acceptance of the value and practice of EIPM and therefore made individual mentoring possible. Those individuals were then able to mentor their colleagues on integrating evidence into their work.
>
> As a result of the one-on-one mentoring, individuals were able to concretely apply EIPM skills to developmental problems in their communities with immediate impact on policy-making and the improvement of service delivery.
>
> Source: Stewart, Langer and Erasmus (2018[26]).

Initiatives to promote engagement and interaction between policy-makers and suppliers of evidence

Policy-makers and professionals are more likely to seek and use research obtained from trusted familiar individuals rather than from formal sources (Oliver et al., 2015[27]; Haynes et al., 2012[28]). Therefore, the different strategies for interaction discussed in the following sections can help to build trusted relationships and increase the opportunities for research to impact policy-making. These approaches include one-off or periodic forums, various platforms for ongoing interactivity and more intensive partnership projects.

Improved engagement between policy-makers and evidence producers, especially when this accomplished in a positive way, can act as a 'virtuous circle' by increasing trust and confidence between the two parties and increasing capacity for shared understanding and collaboration. One-off or periodic forums are generally received by attendees who self-report 'broadened knowledge', but attendance can be uneven, with difficulties engaging senior policy-makers (Haynes et al., 2018[2]). Platforms for ongoing interactivity can help to establish more trusting and equal partnerships between researchers and policy-makers. However, whilst such activities are valued by participants, there can be poor awareness of the purpose and resources available in some of the programmes. Nevertheless, some studies have found self-reported increases in understanding of research use for policy-making.

One-off or periodic interactive forums

Interventions and approaches that bring together policy-makers and researchers include one-off or periodic seminars or forums, such as roundtables, cross-sector retreats and policy dialogues (Haynes et al., 2018[2]). These approaches aim to build mutual interest, trust, respect as well as promoting learning about each other's values, contexts, constraints and practices.

At a European level, the Joint Research Centre of the European Commission has organised an 'Evidence and policy summer school' for a number of years. The summer school aims to help junior to mid-career researchers to have more impact and policy-makers to use evidence for policy solutions. The summer school focuses on the tools and approaches to inform the policy-making process through evidence.

In Australia, engagement between policy-makers and researchers has been promoted through the use of 'Policy Roundtables' described in Box 4.6.

> **Box 4.6. Facilitated engagement between knowledge producers and users: Policy Roundtables in Australia**
>
> - The Australian Primary Health Care Research Institute (APHCRI) is a nationally funded knowledge brokerage organisation.
> - Since 2008 the Institute has organised 'APHCRI conversations' which is a regular programme of roundtable presentations held at the Department of Health to facilitate exchange between APHCRI Network researchers and Department policy-makers. The Roundtables typically involve 10-20 people made up of senior executive officers with the Department of Health and the departments of the Prime Minister and the Cabinet the Treasury and Finance.
> - A knowledge broker facilitates the sessions by identifying subject areas and researchers, determining issues of interest to the Department of Health, and suggesting individuals and areas to receive invitations.
> - The roundtables typically comprise of 30 minutes of presentation and 1 hour of discussion. This is designed to facilitate knowledge translation and exchange by enabling substantive discussion between the knowledge producers and users.
> - Evaluation of the roundtables suggested that they were highly effective in conveying information and in stimulating policy-makers' thinking around a relevant issue. The content of the roundtables was directly relevant to the policy-makers' work and the roundtables established a regular forum for dissemination to a receptive audience of knowledge users.
>
> Source: Dwan, McInnes and Mazumdar (2015[29]) and Australian Primary Health Care Research Institute (2019[30]).

Platforms for ongoing interactivity

Platforms for ongoing interactivity can include communities of practice, formal networks and cross-sector committees. The rationale for such initiatives is that repeated face-to-face contact permits the development of trust, respect and ease of communication. Genuine and sustained collaboration can also increase ownership and investment in the research and dissemination process (Haynes et al., 2018[2]).

More intensive platforms for ongoing activity include the Policy Liaison Initiative for improving the use of Cochrane systematic reviews (Brennan et al., 2016[31]). This involved creating an 'Evidence-Based Policy Network' to facilitate knowledge sharing between policy-makers and researchers, alongside seminars by national and international researchers in the field of evidence synthesis and implementation (see Box 4.7). Poland also has experience in developing platforms for interaction between researchers and policy-makers (Box 4.8).

> **Box 4.7. The Policy Liaison Initiative for improving the use of Cochrane systematic reviews**
>
> The Policy Liaison Initiative (PLI) is a long-term knowledge translation initiative designed to support the use of Cochrane systematic reviews in health policy. A joint initiative between the Australasian Cochrane Centre and Australian Government Department of Health and Ageing, the PLI includes three core elements.
>
> 1. *A community of practice for evidence-informed policy.* This comprised of an Evidence-Based Policy Network to facilitate knowledge sharing between policy-makers and the Cochrane Collaboration. The members of the network receive bulletins alerting them to new and updated reviews, and seminars on evidence synthesis and implementation.
> 2. *Skills building workshops.* These covered a range of topics including types of evidence, research study design and matching, searching for empirical and review evidence, critical appraisal and applying evidence to the local context. The training material and resources from the workshops were made available on the website.
> 3. *A website and summaries of policy-relevant reviews.* A web portal for indexing and accessing policy-relevant Cochrane reviews and summaries was created. A tailored summary format was also created to present the findings of reviews.
>
> Source: Adapted from (Brennan et al., 2016[31]).

In 2009 the Preventing Violence Across the Lifespan (PreVAil) was established as an integrated knowledge translation network to support effective partnerships between its members as well as joint research and application in the area of family violence prevention (Kothari, Sibbald and Wathen, 2014[32]). PreVAil is internal in scope involving 60 researchers and knowledge users from Asia, Australia, Canada, Europe, the UK and the US. PreVAil's approach includes knowledge generation, dissemination and utilisation. The majority of funding, provided by the Canadian Federal Government is used to support attendance at meetings as well as knowledge translation specific activities (Kothari, Sibbald and Wathen, 2014[32]).

> **Box 4.8. The Constitution for Science: the participatory pre-consultation process of reform of the higher education and science system in Poland**
>
> In 2018 a comprehensive systemic reform of the Polish higher education and science system, named the Constitution for Science, entered into force. The impulse behind its introduction came from the academic community, which had a huge influence on the shape of the act. A process of pre-consultation of a draft act lasted almost 800 days and involved approximately 7 000 scientists, students and experts.
>
> The pre-consultation process comprised several elements, two of which were particularly innovative. The first one was the competition for draft guidelines for the new law, which was the initial step of pre-consultation. As a result of the competition, three teams of experts originating from the academic community were selected, whose task was to propose separate concepts for the reform. In order to stimulate a debate on changes in the system, the teams were obliged to carry out their own consultation process, which included i.e. meetings with stakeholders and running surveys, while preparing the policy papers. The outcome of this stage of pre-consultation was three variants of the guidelines, which

provided essential input into a discussion on the reform, both in terms of diagnosis and proposals of changes.

The teams' policy papers served as the starting point for the discussion within the academic community, which was the next part of the pre-consultation. The discussion took the form of a series of events, called the National Congress of Science, which aimed at creating a platform for authentic deliberation involving not only representatives of stakeholders organisations but also individual academics interested in the reform.

Nine conferences were organised in different Polish cities, with each devoted to different areas of higher education and science policy. These conferences were followed by the final Congress, which took place in September 2017 and brought together over two thousand participants. Each event involved numerous panel discussions, workshops and seminars which allowed for active participation by the attendees.

The pre-consultation process was followed by public consultations of the first draft of the reform, which were also exceptionally long: they lasted from September 2017 to January 2018. After endorsing the reform proposal by the Government, the new law on higher education and science was adopted by the Parliament in July 2018.

Partnership projects

Partnership projects include various schemes to bring policy-makers into contact with individual scientists, through collaborating in the development of research projects as well as ad-hoc or formalised systems of parliamentary advice where researchers are called to provide advice.

In 2015, the UK Cabinet Office set up the 'Cross-Government Trial Advice Panel' in partnership with the Economic and Social Research Council. The Trial Advice Panel brings together a team of experts from academia and within the civil service to support the use of experiments in public policy (What Works Network, 2018[33]). The Panel offers the opportunity of sharing expertise, allowing departments with limited knowledge in evaluation to work with departments that do, as well as with top academic experts. In so doing, the Trial Advice Panel aims to reduce the barriers that departments face in commissioning, conducting evaluations, and using the resulting evidence to improve public policies.

The UK has also created a programme that pairs academics and Members of Parliament, described in Box 4.9. In addition, the Open Innovation Team in the Cabinet Office that pairs academics with civil service teams.

> **Box 4.9. The MP and Research Pairing Programme in the UK.**
>
> In the UK, the Centre for Science and Policy created a programme that brings academics and policy-makers together to bridge the gap between the two communities.
>
> In order to build policy-makers' capacity to use research in their work, the pairing programme worked as a long-term intervention that built relationships between policy-makers and researchers.
>
> The pairing programme links policy-makers with a range of experts through 'Policy Fellowships'. The Fellowship connects policy-makers with 25 to 30 researchers from fields relevant to the policy-maker's work. The policy-makers then connect with the researchers on a regular basis.
>
> Through creating these connections, the programme aims to facilitate more dialogue between the two communities, to make research more accessible, and to increase policy-makers' use of evidence in their work.
>
> Source: Newman, Fisher and Shaxson (2012[14]).

The Australian Institute of Family Studies (AIFS) is the government body responsible for the delivery high quality, policy-relevant research on families' wellbeing. AIFS has developed an 'Expert Panel' supporting practitioners in delivering high-quality services for the end-users (Robinson, 2017[34]). The panel gathers experts in research, practice and evaluation, who serve as advisors and facilitators. These experts support practitioners in implementing a policy by measuring outcomes, trying new policy approaches, and conducting research and evaluations.

In Finland, a 'Hack for Society' brings together academics, NGOs as well as national and local government to develop co-creative teams to work on service design, co-creation and societal trials. The goals are to simultaneously strengthen the understanding of different professional roles whilst tackling complex contemporary policy challenges (SITRA, 2017[35]). The Netherlands has also developed an initiative to bring academics into partnership with policy-makers (see Box 4.10).

> **Box 4.10. Establishing evidence-informed policy through partnerships: The Rotterdam Healthy in the City programme**
>
> In 2005, the Netherlands Organization for Health Research and Development started a programme to develop Academic Collaborative Centres (ACC) for Public Health. This was a virtual infrastructure for long-term collaborations between a regional Public Health Service (PHS) and a university research department.
>
> The programme aimed to strengthen the usefulness of scientific research for evidence based policy and practice. Dutch ACCs operate under a collaborative agreement and the exchange of personnel between the PHS and the university.
>
> The Healthy in the City programme was one of the ACC's programmes, initiated after a request by a local representative in the Rotterdam Council to explore the measures necessary to upgrade the health status of the Rotterdam population to the Dutch average level. This established a collaboration between the Department of Public Health at Rotterdam Erasmus MC and the PHS.
>
> A 'Small But Beautiful' procedure was developed to break down common tensions between researchers and policy-makers, such as diverging problem perceptions and timelines. In 3-month research projects, practical policy questions were addressed in interactive rounds of problem clarification and amenability to research, research design, report discussions, and user-focused presentations. The procedure seemed highly promising in fostering two-way interactions.
>
> Source: Adapted from Wehrens, Bekker and Bal (2010[36]).

The US also has a range of different partnership projects in different policy areas. The National Poverty Research Center is a partnership between the US Department of Health and Human Services and the University of Wisconsin-Madison. The Center provides research, training and dissemination to inform policy and practice. The Center creates a space for extensive collaboration among researchers, policy-makers and practitioners (University of Wisconsin-Madison, 2019[37]). Another example of a partnership project is the Quality Enhancement Research Initiative, which includes a policy resource center. The Center provides timely, rigorous data analysis to the government to support the development of policy. The Center brings together stakeholders including practitioners, researchers, policy-makers, service users and the general public (U.S. Department of Veterans Affairs, 2017[38]).

Diagnostic tools to evaluate organisational capacities for EIPM

Evidence-informed policy-making is more likely to occur if organisations have a culture that promotes and values research use and that invests in resources that facilitate staff engagement with research (Makkar et al., 2015[39]; Makkar et al., 2018[40]). Therefore, measures of organisational research use culture and capacity are needed to identifying strengths, areas for improvement and assess the impact of capacity building initiatives. A first step in enabling organisations to increase their ability to identify and assess research and use it in policy-making is to examine the existing organisational capacity to access, interpret and use research findings (Kothari et al., 2009[41]). Furthermore, having tools to assess organisational capacity helps to understand what it is about some agencies or departments that leads them to cultivate and embrace evidence-informed policy-making (Hall and Van Ryzin, 2018[42]).

These tools were less numerous but are designed to promote the capacity to evaluate evidence within the public sector. For example, Canada's Evidence Literacy diagnostic tool is a self-assessment tool to enable service managers and policy organisations to help them understand their capacity to acquire assess, adapt and apply research (Kothari et al., 2009[41]). The tool is organised into four general areas, with a number of questions addressing performance in each area (see Box 4.11). The tool is envisaged as a catalyst for discussions about research use, thus encouraging and supporting EIPM.

> **Box 4.11. Is research working for you? Questions addressed by the Evidence Literacy diagnostic tool**
>
> - Acquire – can the organisation find and obtain the research findings?
> - Assess – can the organisation assess research findings to ensure they are reliable, relevant and applicable to its context?
> - Adapt – can the organisation present the research to decision makers in a useful way
> - Apply – are there skills, structures, processes and a culture in the organisation to promote and use research findings in decision making
>
> Source: Kothari et al. (2009[41]).

The US developed tool called 'Norm of Evidence and Research in Decision-making' (NERD) that can be used across organizational and functional settings to assess evidence based management practices within an agency (Hall and Van Ryzin, 2018[42]).. Its development was motivated by the thought that organisations seeking to use evidence in policy-making must be aware of their organisation's norms of evidence use, and differences that may exist across divisions, in order to be most effective. In terms of its practical application in policy organisations, NERD could be used to make staffing decisions to improve person-organisation fit agency (Hall and Van Ryzin, 2018[42]).

The Organisational Research Access, Culture and Leadership (ORACLe) tool is a theory-based measure of organisational capacity to engage with and use research in policy development (Makkar et al., 2015[39]). ORACLe assesses multiple dimensions of organisational capacity including the systems, supports and tools that organisations have in place to use research, as well as the values placed on research within an organisation. It is administered as a structured interview with organisational leaders (see Box 4.12). A key advantage and use of the scoring system produced is that it enables organisations to identify specific areas for development and determines their strategic importance. (Makkar et al., 2017[5]).

> **Box 4.12. The ORACLe Interview Questions**
>
> - Does your organisation have documented processes for how policies should be developed?
> - Do these processes encourage or require staff to use research in policy development?
> - Are programmes available for leaders to improve their confidence or expertise in the use of research in policy-making? (Leaders mean any level of executive or management or anyone else with a formal or informal leadership role.)
> - Do the position descriptions or performance management systems for senior policy-makers in your organisation cover expertise in the use of research in policy-making?
> - In the last 6 months, have leaders of your organisation referred to research in their internal communication (e.g. newsletters, bulletins, updates, tweets, etc.)?
> - Does your organisation provide access to training for staff in how to access research, appraise and apply research for policy development/implementation/evaluation?
>
> Source: Makkar et al. (2015[39]).

Initiatives to build organisational capacities for evidence-informed policy-making

The use of evidence is intimately linked to organisational structures and systems. Undertaking changes to improve use therefore requires reflection on where evidence advice can enter the system and how strong or well-integrated evidence structures should be (Parkhurst, 2017[43]). These considerations introduce complex human dynamics that need to be considered in the development and implementation of strategies, including organisational culture and the nature and quality of communication within the organisation (Damschroder et al., 2009[44]). This suggests that the participatory development of organisational and system level interventions may offer the best chance of success (Haynes et al., 2018[2]).

The hypothesised mechanisms of changes to organisational structures and systems are complex and manifold cutting across the full range of skill competencies identified in the OECD/JRC framework. For example, organisational systems both serve the delivery of organisations' routine practices but also signal their values. Workforce development can help to provide further opportunities for staff and incentives which can be motivating. The creation of in-house research roles and other resources also signal managerial commitment to research use. Although the different organisational improvements discussed in this chapter have different purposes, they can all help to embed research use and drive a culture of evidence use in policy organisations. In terms of the COM-B model, these organisational factors can be understood as providing the incentives, which motivate the individual to use evidence (or not). Organisational factors also enhance or constrain opportunities for individuals to use evidence. A summary of the organisational initiatives is presented in Box 4.13 with full details of the initiatives in the Appendix.

> **Box 4.13. Summary of organisational initiatives to facilitate the use of evidence**
>
> Improving organisational tools, resources and processes
>
> - Whole of government and ministry level strategies for EIPM e.g. Ireland's 'Evidence into Policy Project
> - Toolkits to support the use of evidence e.g. INASP's EIPM toolkit
>
> Improving organisational infrastructure e.g. the US the Foundations for Evidence-Based Policy-making Act
>
> Establishing strategic units to support an evidence-informed approach
>
> - Cross government units on what works, experimentation and evaluation e.g. Austria's Federal Performance Management Office
> - Dedicated analytical professions and units with miniseries and departments e.g. Chile's Dedicated technical support for performance management

Improving organisational tools, resources and processes

A range of organisational tools, resources and processes have been implemented to facilitate the use of research within policy organisations. These include toolkits, knowledge management protocols, organisational strategies and evaluation frameworks, and dedicated funds for commissioning research.

The New Zealand Policy Project was launched in 2014 to improve the quality of policy advice being produced across government agencies (Washington and Mintrom, 2018[45]). It deployed policy analytic tools and frameworks to investigate current practice in policy design to improve the quality of policy advice across the whole of government. A key aim was to ensure that policy advice was developed on the basis of the best available evidence and insights, including an understanding of 'what works'. This included developing a 'Policy Methods Toolbox', which is a repository of policy development methods that helps policy practitioners identify and select the right approach for their policy initiative Box 4.15.

In Germany, the federal government began a systematic evaluation of all major regulatory instruments at the end of 2014 as part of their Programme of Work for Better Regulation. The implementation of systemic evaluations aimed to strengthen performance management by evaluating the effectiveness of programmes at achieving their intended goals. The reforms were designed to enable the government to identify what works and what does not (OECD, 2016[17]).

In Ireland, the Research and Evaluation Unit in the Department for Children and Youth Affairs developed the 'Evidence into Policy Programme', which aims to support governmental policy priorities through research and knowledge transfer activities to promote the uptake and use of evidence to drive policy change (Box 4.14).

> **Box 4.14. Ireland's Evidence Into Policy Programme**
>
> The Department for Children and Youth Affairs developed the 'Evidence into Policy Programme', which aims to support governmental policy priorities through research and knowledge transfer activities to promote the uptake and use of evidence to drive policy change. The Programme involves a number or interrelated strands, including the following:

- Guidance notes on research-related matters. These guidance notes provide advice and information on key stages of the research to policy process, in support of evidence-informed policy-making. The first guidance note 'The Need for Research' sets out the need for research, including: 1) why it is important; 2) what it is; 3) how to implement formal research.
- A Research and Evaluation Unit Newsletter. This is a mechanism to raise the profile, activities and supports available from the REU; to share knowledge and information; and in particular, to highlight resources available to policy units and increase the demand for evidence.
- Request for evidence support. This is a mechanism for policy units to reflect on their priority policy concerns with research and evidence needs. The intention is that this will embed a mutual annual business planning process between policy units and the evidence unit, such that research and evidence production, and efforts to promote uptake and use, become core business deliverables.
- A dedicated research and evaluation framework agreement. This will create a pre-selected panel of research services providers with subject matter and methodological expertise as relevant to five national strategies on which DCYA has lead responsibility. This should enable the production of robust, policy-relevant commissioned research to answer specific policy questions.

In the UK, the Department for Environment, Food and Rural Affairs (DEFRA) has published a number of iterations of an Evidence Investment Strategy, which aims to embed an evidence-informed strategy across the department and the wider sector (Shaxson, 2019[46]; DEFRA, 2010[47]). The Evidence Investment Strategy sets out DEFRA's priorities for sourcing evidence, the aims of its evidence work, the evidence needs across the organisation and describes a framework that DEFRA uses to allocate its evidence resources. Underpinning this is a strategy to retain capabilities such as infrastructure, networks, staff and expertise, and data to enable the department to respond to emergencies, alongside crosscutting capabilities.

Box 4.15. Policy Methods Toolbox in New Zealand

- The Policy Methods Toolbox was developed in New Zealand and is a repository of policy development methods that helps policy practitioners identify and select the right approach for their policy initiatives.
- The Toolbox emerged from the Policy Project that the New Zealand government started in 2014. The Policy Project was established to improve the quality of policy advice across the government. The government recognised that there was a need to improve the evidence-base of their policy advice and to better design policies and programmes around the needs of users. The project resulted in the Policy Methods Toolbox.
- The Toolbox includes a variety of resources including tools, guides and case studies. The Toolbox is divided into four major themes: Start Right, Behavioural Insights, Design Thinking and Public Participation.
- The Toolbox provides concrete steps and actions that policy-makers can take to improve the policy-making process through making better use of research and science, using meta-data, feedback loops and input from frontline operational staff and various forms of evaluation.

Source: Department of the Prime Minister and Cabinet (2017[48]).

In Canada, the province of Ontario has been at the forefront of developing organisational initiatives to improve the quality of evidence-informed policy-making in the field of public health. One of these initiatives is described in Box 4.16.

> **Box 4.16. Building organisational capacity for EIPM in public health in Ontario**
>
> In Ontario, Canada, the public health sector undertook the initiative to increase their use of evidence in policy-making through a variety of methods. Prior to this, there was no organizational-wide formalised and standardised methods, tools or expectations on how evidence is to be used in decision-making.
>
> The public health organisation invested in nurturing a culture and developing the tools, processes and structures that would support, sustain and increase EIDM. These efforts included: offering training and skills enhancement workshops; developing/selecting methods and tools for conducting literature reviews; creating clubs and other forums for sharing knowledge; restructuring the library and expanding its service capacity; creating and supplementing EIDM-related positions; accessing external expertise; commissioning literature reviews; and committing significant base budget funding to EIDM.
>
> The public health organisation found that in order to build capacity for EIDM, they needed to focus on the tasks and resources required to conduct evidence reviews, as well as, identify and respond to the needs of decision makers.
>
> Source: Adapted from Peirson et al (2012[49]).

Institutionalising the use of evidence – the contribution of OECD's Survey of Monitoring and Policy Evaluation

The OECD is developing a comprehensive view of the institutionalisation and use of policy evaluation across OECD countries, based on a survey of policy evaluation (Beuselinck et al., 2018[50]; OECD, 2018[51]). The institutionalisation of policy evaluation includes the enactment and implementation of regulations, evaluation policies, as well as the specific institutional arrangements within the government (Jacob, Speer and Furubo, 2015[52]). Given that the underpinning rationale for policy evaluation different among countries, so does the approach to institutionalisation. Some countries, such as France and Switzerland, have the use of evaluations embedded in their constitutions. Other countries, such as Austria, Germany and the United States, have framed evaluation as part of larger public management reforms. Furthermore, several countries have recently introduced - or are currently in the process of introducing - important changes to their institutional set-up and/or underpinning legal and policy framework, some of which are described in the sections that follow.

Toolkits to support the use of evidence

The OECD's Observatory for Public Sector Innovation (OPSI) has created a Toolkit Navigator that contains a wide variety of tools for public sector innovation and transformation. OPSI created this database because they found that there are a plethora of free innovation toolkits and guides that exist to help people identify, develop and practice necessary skills and apply new ways of reaching an outcome. So OPSI created the Navigator to help people easily find the tools they need. Within this database, there are many evidence-informed policy-making toolkits that also address the needs of policy-makers wanting to increase their use of evidence in their work. The Quality of Administration Toolbox is an important tool developed at European level by the Joint Research Centre (see Box 4.17).

INASP has also created a toolkit for evidence-informed policy-making. INASP is an organisation that works with a global network of partners to strengthen the capacity of individuals and institutions to produce, share and use research and knowledge, in support of national development. The Toolkit focuses on building skills in finding, evaluating and communicating evidence as well as developing practical implementation plans. The Toolkit is designed as a training programme that includes a trainers' manual, handouts, activities, presentations and readings (INASP, 2018[53]). Based on work done with the South African Department of Environmental Affairs, the Overseas Development Institute (ODI) has produced guidelines and good practices for evidence-informed policy-making in a government department, which are designed to underpin a systematic approach to improving EIPM within a government department. (Wills, 2016[54]).

> **Box 4.17. Quality of Public Administration: A Toolbox for Practitioners**
>
> - The Quality of Public Administration: A Toolbox for Practitioners, written by the Joint Research Centre (JRC) of the European Commission, explores the qualities of good policy-making and approaches to longer-term strategic planning.
> - The JRC is the European Commission's science and knowledge service. It employs scientists to carry out research in order to provide independent scientific advice and support to EU policy. The JRC created this Toolbox to provide tools to EU governments that can assist in strengthening their policy-making.
> - The Toolbox emphasises the importance of systematic feedback, external scrutiny and innovation within the public sector. Throughout, the Toolbox discusses the importance of the use of research in policy-making and details how data analytics can help overcome the challenge of designing better informed policies that reflect and address the complexity of policy problems.
> - The Toolbox provides resources for all stages of the policy process. The Toolbox provides practical steps for how to use data analysis to uncover trends, patterns and connections that might otherwise be invisible.
>
> Source: European Commission (2017[55]).

Improving the knowledge and data infrastructure

In recognition of the limitations in infrastructure and capacity to support the use of evidence, some jurisdictions have launched initiatives to try and maximise the use of government's existing assets for EIPM. This can include library facilities, research portals and clearinghouses as well as data sharing software and other methods of maximising government's data assets.

In the US, the Foundations for Evidence-Based Policy-making Act was designed to ensure that the necessary data quality and review structures were in place to support the use of administrative data in evaluations (see Box 4.18).

> **Box 4.18. The Foundations for Evidence-based policy-making in the US**
>
> In the US, the federal government sought to increase the use of evidence in policy-making across all federal agencies. Some agencies were already excellent at using evidence while others lacked the skills or capacity necessary.
>
> In 2017, the Foundations for Evidence-Based Policy-making bill has since been passed into law. The reforms proposed in the bill will expand upon existing capabilities and push agencies to adopt stronger practices that would generate more evidence about what works and what needs improvement. The data collected by agencies will also be more accessible across agencies and to external groups for research purposes. At the same time, the protection of individuals' privacy will be increased.
>
> In order to increase capacity, Federal agencies are being asked to appoint senior official responsible for coordinating the agency's evaluation activities, learning agenda and information reported to the Office of Management and Budget (OMB) on evidence; establish and utilize multi-year learning agendas; document the resources dedicated to program evaluation; and improve the quality of the information provided to OMB on evidence-building activities.

The OECD has been working on projects focused on creating a data-driven culture in the public sector in order to better use data to support policy-making, and service design and delivery. These have been prepared in the area of digital government, budgeting and integrity.

In the US, the Government has made a commitment to open data and data governance. The Government has a number of initiatives to facilitate that including the website Data.org that provides data to the public and features over 188 000 datasets on topics such as education, public safety, health care, energy and agriculture. To assist agencies in their open data efforts and to support the Federal open data ecosystem, the Administration has also built additional resources such as Project Open Data, which provides agencies with tools and best practices to make their data publicly available, and the Project Open Data Dashboard, which is used to provide the public a quarterly evaluation of agency open data progress. With these data available, the public is able to assess the work of the government agencies, compare the impact of programmes and hold government accountable (OECD, 2016[17]). These initiatives are further supported by the Foundations for Evidence-Based Policy-making, which assists agencies to increase their capacity to generate and use evidence in their policy-making.

Establishing strategic positions and units to support an evidence-informed approach and the capacity to use evidence.

A number of governments across the OECD have appointed Chief Scientific Advisors to support the government in ensuring that the systems are in place within the government for managing and using scientific research. In the UK, the Government Chief Science Advisor's (GCSA) role is to advise the Prime Minister and Cabinet on science, engineering and technology. The GCSA reports directly to the Cabinet Secretary and works closely with the Science Minister, and other ministers and permanent secretaries across Whitehall. In addition, the majority of UK government departments also have Department Chief Scientific Advisers (DCSA's). The DCSA works alongside the government analytical professions, ministers and the policy profession to ensure that evidence is at the core of decisions made within the department. This can include the provision of advice directly to the secretary of state and oversight of the systems for ensuring that policy-makers consider relevant evidence in policy-making (Government Office for Science, 2015[56]).

New Zealand is another OECD country that has both a GCSE role, alongside DCSA roles. For example, the Ministry for Social Development has a DCSA who works to improve the use of evidence in policy development and advice. Ireland and Australia also both have GCSA role. In Australia, the GCSA also holds the position of Executive Officer of the Commonwealth Science Council to identify challenges and opportunities for Australia that can be addressed using science. They also advocate for Australian science internationally and are a key communicator of science to the general public, with the aim to promote understanding of, contribution to and enjoyment of science and evidence-based thinking.

Establishing strategic units to support an evidence-informed approach

Cross government units on what works, experimentation and evaluation

A number of OECD countries have established dedicated teams to champion the developing and evaluation of new approaches to public sector delivery, whilst ensuring that the government has the skills and capacity to use the evidence that is generated. In the UK, a dedicated team within the Cabinet Office supports the government's 'What Works Approach' (see Box 4.19). In the US, a dedicated Evidence Team within the Office of Management and Budget (OMB) acts a central hub of expertise across the federal government, working with other OMB offices in order to set research priorities and ensure the use of appropriate evaluation methodologies in federal evaluations. The Evidence Team also works actively to ensure the findings from research and other forms of evidence are used in policy design, by developing agency capacity to generate and use evidence and providing technical assistance and other initiatives to a wide range of Federal agencies and functions. Complementing the work of OMB, the Office of Evaluation Sciences in the General Services Administration that works across the federal government to support trials and impact evaluations.

Box 4.19. The UK's What Works Approach

The UK's What Works initiative aims to improve the way government and other organisations create, share and use (or 'generate, translate and adopt') high quality evidence for decision-making. It supports more effective and efficient services across the public sector at national and local levels. The What Works Network is made up of seven independent What Works Centres and four affiliate members.

A What Works National Adviser located in the Cabinet Office promotes and supports the independent What Works Network and carry out the following cross-cutting initiatives:

- running a Cross-Government Trial Advice Panel, with experts from across academia and government providing a free service for all civil servants to help test whether policies and programmes are working
- sharing findings from the What Works Centres across government and promoting discussion on 'what works'
- supporting the development of a civil service with the skills, capability and commitment to use evidence effectively
- helping policy-makers to make informed judgements on investment in services that lead to impact and value for money for citizens.

The Italian government has also sought to strengthen accountability through better performance management and evaluation. The Office for the Programme of Government of the Prime Minister's Office monitors and assesses progress on the implementation of the Government programme (OECD, 2016[17]). When a monitoring exercise shows challenges towards achieving a particular goal, the Office offers support and encouragement to the relevant administration. In Austria, the Federal Performance Management Office plays a comparable role in strengthening accountability through performance management and evaluation (Box 4.20).

Box 4.20. Austria's Federal Performance Management Office

- The Austrian government has developed a government wide approach to performance management and evaluation, supported by key central government agencies and offices.
- Since 2013 Austria's Federal Constitution commits the government to outcome-orientated goals as a principle of performance management. Regulatory impact assessments are used to implement outcome-orientated budgeting in both the policy-making and evaluation process. All new laws, regulations and bigger projects are discussed on the basis of their desired outcomes.
- Performance information is also contained in the annual Federal Budget, with results evaluated every year by line ministries, so that deviations from plans can be detected and steps taken to get progress back on track. The Federal Performance Management Office at the Federal Chancellery ensures the collaboration of line ministries and uses a web-based database and evaluation tool.
- Evaluation results are used to identify the potential for increasing the effectiveness and efficiency of the public administration, by taking into account the results from evaluation when developing the next strategic plan. Evaluation results are also observed and commented on by the federal court of audit and discussed by the national parliament as a critical part of the annual budget process.

Source: Adapted from OECD (2016[17]).

In Korea, the Government Performance Evaluation Committee was established in 2013 as part of the Office for Government Policy Co-ordination (OPC) inside the Prime Minister's Secretariat. The goal of the committee is to evaluate the policies of central government agencies on an annual basis. The Government Performance Evaluation system was established by the OPC to focus government efforts on resolving issues concerning the Presidential Agenda in a timely fashion (OECD, 2016[17]).

The Japanese government has implemented a number of initiatives to improve the execution and use of policy evaluation across government (Box 4.21).

> **Box 4.21. Japan's Policy Evaluation Council to strengthen government use of policy evaluation**
>
> In 2013 'Guidelines for Performance Evaluation' were developed in order to enhance the use of results of evaluations for policy and budget reviews, as well as to improve public accountability.
>
> In 2015, the Policy Evaluation Council was established under the Ministry of Internal Affairs and Communications (MIC), with the goal of improving the quality of policy evaluation, such as by developing logic models associated with evaluations.
>
> To ensure the rigorous implementation of policy evaluations the Administrative Evaluation Bureau (AEB) review the policy evaluations carried out by ministries, identifying elements that need to be improved and publicising the reports and the responses by ministries. The AEB also carries our evaluations involving two or more ministries, which would be challenging for an individual ministry to carry out.
>
> The MIC also prepares an annual report on the status of policy evaluation carried out by the ministries and how the results of evaluations have been reflected in policy planning and the development process. Finally, MIC aggregates results of policy evaluation by ministries on the 'Portal Site for Policy Evaluation'.
>
> Source: Adapted from OECD (2016[17])

In Spain, the State Agency for the Evaluation of Public Policy and Service Quality (AEVAL) was created in 2007, as part of the Office of the State Secretary of Public Administration to evaluate the ministries in the government through reports on quality management activities on an annual basis. AEVAL also pooled the best practices across the government into a repertoire of good practices that ministries could use as benchmarks to compare themselves against. In the same way, AEVAL performed an evaluation of public policies commissioned by the Government. Following a change of government in 2017, AEVAL was disbanded with the General Directorate of Public Governance (within the Secretary of State of Civil Service) taking ownership of the evaluation of the quality of the services, whereas the new Institute for the Evaluation of Public Policies (IEPP) was created as a renewed commitment of the Government in matters of evaluation of public policies.

The Institute for the Evaluation of Public Policies is working on the development of methodologies for good practices in evaluation through the drafting of guides that will serve as support to the different agencies to carry out evaluations. In addition, this body promotes training for public employees thanks to a training plan on evaluation and specific formative actions in different levels of Government. The Institute advises on evaluability of the plans and programs during the planning stage and it is in charge of several strategic plans to carry out the ex-post evaluation.

Mexico has a similar body called the National Council for the Evaluation for Social Development Policy (CONEVAL), which is a decentralised public body of the Federal Public Administration. CONEVAL has the autonomy and technical capacity to generate objective information and evaluations of social policy, which then feeds back into the policy-making process to foster better policies.

Colombia has also created a National Monitoring and Evaluation system, described in Box 4.22.

> **Box 4.22. Colombia's National Monitoring and Evaluation System**
>
> The Ministry of Planning (Departamento Nacional de Planeación-DNP) is a technical entity in charge leading, coordinating and articulating the medium and long-term planning for the sustainable and inclusive development of the country.
>
> The remit of the DNP includes
>
> - advises the President and entities of the National Government and support other state entities in the construction and implementation of policies,
> - coordinating the implementation of the government programme to ensure compliance with its priorities and articulation with a long-term vision, and
> - promoting the effectiveness of public investment policies and projects based on monitoring and evaluation.
>
> To support these functions, the DNP created the Sistema Nacional de Evaluación de Gestión y Resultados- SINERGIA, which manages the national monitoring and evaluation system, supports the follow-up process, and designs and carry out evaluations of key government programs.
>
> SINERGIA, under the lead of DNP, is not only recognized as one of the major information sources in terms of evaluations, follow-ups, and technical support of public policies, but also as an agent of transparency in the public sector.
>
> Under a continuous collection and analysis of data, the *territorial monitoring* allows to determinate, periodically, the achievements and challenges in terms of the National Development Plan (Plan de Nacional de Desarrollo-PND).
>
> Source: adapted from OECD (2016[17]).

Other central initiatives have been created in response to calls for greater experimentation, whilst also often encompassing wider issues of evidence generation and use within government. In Canada, the government introduced a commitment to devote a fixed percentage of programme funds towards innovation (Government of Canada, 2016[57]) which was part of the government's overall focus on evidence based policy-making; results and delivery (see Box 4.23). This drive is supported by an Innovation and Experimentation Team in the Treasury Board to provide central support by ensuring the enabling factors are in place to support experimentation; by helping to build capacity; by providing practical tools and resources; and by leveraging existing platforms and reporting structures so that departments can track and share experiences and showcase success.

> **Box 4.23. Experimentation direction for Deputy Heads – December 2016**
>
> In December 2016, the Treasury Board Secretariat and the Privy Council Office issued a direction reinforcing the Government's commitment to devote a fixed percentage of programme funds to experimenting, and providing context and directions for Deputy Heads on how to implement this commitment.
>
> The direction defines experimentation as testing new approaches to learn what works and what does not work using a rigorous method that could feature:
>
> 1. deliberate, thoughtful, and ethical experimental design;
> 2. comparisons between interventions and base cases to capture evidence (e.g. randomized controlled trials, A/B testing, counterfactual experiments, baseline performance data, pre- and post-tests);
> 3. randomized assignment to test and control groups, whenever possible;
> 4. rigorous impact measurement and causality assessment; and
> 5. transparent publication of positive, negative and neutral results.
>
> Source: OECD (2018[58]).

Dedicated analytical professions and units with ministries and departments

A further organisational strategy that has been implemented by a number of governments has been to establish internal research support bodies, such as research units and committees. Co-location and control over expertise in-house are likely to increase policy relevance, applicability and timeliness of evidence for decision-making. The availability of in-house research expertise also facilitates opportunities and incentives that may motivate policy-makers to use evidence their work (Haynes et al., 2018[2]).

Some OECD countries have developed dedicated analytical professions to support evidence-informed policy-making. In the UK, a total of 15,000 analysts are based across the government departments. These analysts belong to a number of analytical professions including the Government Economic Service, the Government Statistical Service and the Government Social Research Service. In Ireland, the Irish Government Economic and Evaluation Service (IGEES) operates as an integrated, cross-Government service, supporting better policy formulation and implementation in the civil service through economic analysis and evaluation. The aim of the IGEES is to contribute to the better design and targeting of Government policy and better outcomes for citizens, by building on existing analytical work and playing a lead role in policy analysis. IGEES operates as a cross-government service, with staff embedded in each Department adding their skill set to the varied expertise working on policy analysis and formulation. IGEES supports and builds economic and evaluation capacity and consistency across the civil service (IGEES, 2014[59]).

In the US, the recent Foundations for Evidence-Based Policy-Making Act requires agencies to create three new positions: Chief Evaluation Officer, Chief Statistical Official, and Chief Data Officer. It also requires the creation of a new (or enhancement of an existing) job series in the civil service for program evaluation.

In Chile, a dedicated system of technical support has been created to support better performance management and evaluation Box 4.24.

> **Box 4.24. Chile's Dedicated technical support for better performance management and evaluation**
>
> Chile's central government has been evaluating its programmes and policies through its System for Programme Evaluation since 2003. The System focuses on three types of ex-post evaluations: evaluations of governmental programmes, programmes impact evaluations and new programme evaluations.
>
> The System for Programme Evaluations makes public the results of its analysis through the Budget Directorate's website. Through an online portal, the public can also access geo-referenced information in order to promote citizen-driven accountability by providing reliable and timely information to the public that is useful for analysing and monitoring resources invested in public works.
>
> The System for Programme Evaluation works to ensure that the data collected across the different sections of the government is useable and comparable in order to do their own evaluations as well as for the public to be able to use.
>
> Source: Adapted from OECD (2016[17])

References

Affairs, P. and A. Institute (eds.) (2016), *Guidelines and good practices for evidence-informed policymaking*. [54]

Australian Primary Health Care Research Institute (2019), *Conversations with APHCRI | Research School of Population Health*, https://rsph.anu.edu.au/research/centres-departments/australian-primary-health-care-research-institute/conversations-with-aphcri (accessed on 23 January 2019). [30]

Beuselinck, E. et al. (2018), *Institutionalisation of Policy Evaluation as Enabler for Sound Public Governance: towards an OECD Perspective*. [50]

Brennan, S. et al. (2016), "Design and formative evaluation of the Policy Liaison Initiative: a long-term knowledge translation strategy to encourage and support the use of Cochrane systematic reviews for informing health policy", *Evidence & Policy: A Journal of Research, Debate and Practice*, Vol. 12/1, pp. 25-52, http://dx.doi.org/10.1332/174426415X14291899424526. [31]

Brennan, S. et al. (2017), "Development and validation of SEER (Seeking, Engaging with and Evaluating Research): a measure of policymakers' capacity to engage with and use research", *Health Research Policy and Systems*, Vol. 15/1, p. 1, http://dx.doi.org/10.1186/s12961-016-0162-8. [3]

Campbell, D. et al. (2011), "Evidence Check: knowledge brokering to commission research reviews for policy", *Evidence & Policy: A Journal of Research, Debate and Practice*, Vol. 7/1, pp. 97-107, http://dx.doi.org/10.1332/174426411X553034. [10]

Damschroder, L. et al. (2009), "Fostering implementation of health services research findings into practice: a consolidated framework for advancing implementation science", *Implementation Science*, Vol. 4/1, p. 50, http://dx.doi.org/10.1186/1748-5908-4-50. [44]

DEFRA (2010), *Defra's Evidence Investment Strategy and beyond*, Department for Environment, Food and Rural Affairs, https://assets.publishing.service.gov.uk/government/uploads/system/uploads/attachment_data/file/69292/pb13346-eis-100126.pdf (accessed on 4 February 2019). [47]

Department of the Prime Minister and Cabinet (2017), *Policy Methods Toolbox*, https://dpmc.govt.nz/our-programmes/policy-project/policy-methods-toolbox-0 (accessed on 29 January 2019). [48]

Dobbins, M. et al. (2009), "A randomized controlled trial evaluating the impact of knowledge translation and exchange strategies", *Implementation Science*, Vol. 4/1, p. 61, http://dx.doi.org/10.1186/1748-5908-4-61. [7]

Dwan, K., P. McInnes and S. Mazumdar (2015), "Measuring the success of facilitated engagement between knowledge producers and users: a validated scale", *Evidence & Policy: A Journal of Research, Debate and Practice*, Vol. 11/2, pp. 239-252, http://dx.doi.org/10.1332/174426414X14165029835102. [29]

EPPI Centre (2016), *Department of Health and Social Care Reviews Facility to support national policy development and implementation*, https://eppi.ioe.ac.uk/cms/Default.aspx?tabid=73 (accessed on 5 February 2019). [11]

EU Science Hub (2019), *Lunchtime science lectures | EU Science Hub*, https://ec.europa.eu/jrc/en/lunchtime-science-lectures (accessed on 5 February 2019). [12]

EU Science Hub (2019), *Science meets Parliaments in Brussels and across Europe*, https://ec.europa.eu/jrc/en/science-meets-parliamentscience-meets-regions (accessed on 22 January 2020). [23]

European Commission (2017), *Quality of Public Administration - A Toolbox for Practitioners*, https://ec.europa.eu/social/main.jsp?catId=738&langId=en&pubId=8055&type=2&furtherPubs=no (accessed on 7 February 2019). [55]

Government of Canada (2016), *Experimentation direction for Deputy Heads - December 2016 - Canada.ca*, https://www.canada.ca/en/innovation-hub/services/reports-resources/experimentation-direction-deputy-heads.html (accessed on 22 January 2019). [57]

Government Office for Science (2015), *Chief Scientific Advisers and their officials: an introduction*, https://assets.publishing.service.gov.uk/government/uploads/system/uploads/attachment_data/file/426307/15-2-chief-scientific-advisers-and-officials-introduction.pdf (accessed on 28 January 2019). [56]

Hall, J. and G. Van Ryzin (2018), "A Norm of Evidence and Research in Decision-making (NERD): Scale Development, Reliability, and Validity", *Public Administration Review*, http://dx.doi.org/10.1111/puar.12995. [42]

Haynes, A. et al. (2012), "Identifying Trustworthy Experts: How Do Policymakers Find and Assess Public Health Researchers Worth Consulting or Collaborating With?", *PLoS ONE*, Vol. 7/3, p. e32665, http://dx.doi.org/10.1371/journal.pone.0032665. [28]

Haynes, A. et al. (2018), "What can we learn from interventions that aim to increase policy-makers' capacity to use research? A realist scoping review", *Health Research Policy and Systems*, Vol. 16/1, p. 31, http://dx.doi.org/10.1186/s12961-018-0277-1. [2]

IGEES (2014), *Irish Government Economic and Evaluation Service*, https://igees.gov.ie/ (accessed on 28 January 2019). [59]

INASP (2018), *Evidence-Informed Policy Making (EIPM) Toolkit | INASP*, https://www.inasp.info/publications/evidence-informed-policy-making-eipm-toolkit (accessed on 8 February 2019). [53]

INGSA (2019), *About – INGSA*, https://www.ingsa.org/about/ (accessed on 7 February 2019). [22]

Jacob, S., S. Speer and J. Furubo (2015), "The institutionalization of evaluation matters: Updating the International Atlas of Evaluation 10 years later", *Evaluation*, Vol. 21/1, pp. 6-31, http://dx.doi.org/10.1177/1356389014564248. [52]

Kauffeld-Monz, M. and M. Fritsch (2013), "Who Are the Knowledge Brokers in Regional Systems of Innovation? A Multi-Actor Network Analysis", *Regional Studies*, Vol. 47/5, pp. 669-685, http://dx.doi.org/10.1080/00343401003713365. [13]

Kothari, A. et al. (2009), "Is research working for you? validating a tool to examine the capacity of health organizations to use research", *Implementation Science*, Vol. 4/1, p. 46, http://dx.doi.org/10.1186/1748-5908-4-46. [41]

Kothari, A., S. Sibbald and C. Wathen (2014), "Evaluation of partnerships in a transnational family violence prevention network using an integrated knowledge translation and exchange model: a mixed methods study", *Health Research Policy and Systems*, Vol. 12/1, p. 25, http://dx.doi.org/10.1186/1478-4505-12-25. [32]

Langer, L., J. Tripney and D. Gough (2016), *The science of using science: researching the use of Research evidence in decision-making.*. [6]

Makkar, S. et al. (2018), "Organisational capacity and its relationship to research use in six Australian health policy agencies", http://dx.doi.org/10.1371/journal.pone.0192528. [40]

Makkar, S. et al. (2015), "The development of ORACLe: a measure of an organisation's capacity to engage in evidence-informed health policy", *Health Research Policy and Systems*, Vol. 14/1, p. 4, http://dx.doi.org/10.1186/s12961-015-0069-9. [39]

Makkar, S. et al. (2017), "Preliminary testing of the reliability and feasibility of SAGE: a system to measure and score engagement with and use of research in health policies and programs", *Implementation Science*, Vol. 12/1, p. 149, http://dx.doi.org/10.1186/s13012-017-0676-7. [5]

Newman, K., C. Fisher and L. Shaxson (2012), "Stimulating Demand for Research Evidence: What Role for Capacity-building?", *IDS Bulletin*, Vol. 43/5, pp. 17-24, http://dx.doi.org/10.1111/j.1759-5436.2012.00358.x. [14]

OECD (2018), *Mapping the knowledge broker function across the OECD*, OECD, Paris. [9]

OECD (2018), *Survey on Policy Evaluation*, OECD, Paris, https://one.oecd.org/#/document/GOV/PGC(2017)29/ANN1/REV1/en?_k=uqglaz (accessed on 5 December 2018). [51]

OECD (2018), *The Innovation System of the Public Service of Canada*, OECD Publishing, Paris, https://dx.doi.org/10.1787/9789264307735-en. [58]

OECD (2017), *National Schools of Government: Building Civil Service Capacity*, OECD Public Governance Reviews, OECD Publishing, Paris, https://dx.doi.org/10.1787/9789264268906-en. [19]

OECD (2016), *Engaging Public Employees for a High-Performing Civil Service*, OECD Public Governance Reviews, OECD Publishing, Paris, https://dx.doi.org/10.1787/9789264267190-en. [15]

OECD (2016), *The Governance of Inclusive Growth: An Overview of Country Initiatives*, OECD Publishing, Paris, https://dx.doi.org/10.1787/9789264265189-en. [17]

OECD (2012), *Capacity Building Seminar on Regulatory Impact Assessment (RIA) - OECD*, http://www.oecd.org/gov/regulatory-policy/riaseminar.htm (accessed on 12 February 2019). [20]

Oliver, K. et al. (2015), "Identifying public health policymakers' sources of information: comparing survey and network analyses", *The European Journal of Public Health*, Vol. 27/suppl_2, p. ckv083, http://dx.doi.org/10.1093/eurpub/ckv083. [27]

Oliver, K. et al. (2014), "A systematic review of barriers to and facilitators of the use of evidence by policymakers", *BMC Health Services Research*, Vol. 14/1, http://dx.doi.org/10.1186/1472-6963-14-2. [1]

Parkhurst, J. (2017), *The politics of evidence : from evidence-based policy to the good governance of evidence*, Routledge, London, http://researchonline.lshtm.ac.uk/3298900/ (accessed on 23 November 2018). [43]

Parra-Cardona, R. et al. (2018), "Strengthening a Culture of Prevention in Low- and Middle-Income Countries: Balancing Scientific Expectations and Contextual Realities", *Prevention Science*, pp. 1-11, http://dx.doi.org/10.1007/s11121-018-0935-0. [18]

Peirson, L. et al. (2012), "Building capacity for evidence informed decision making in public health: a case study of organizational change", *BMC Public Health*, Vol. 12/1, p. 137, http://dx.doi.org/10.1186/1471-2458-12-137. [49]

R. Makkar, S. et al. (2016), "The development of SAGE: A tool to evaluate how policymakers' engage with and use research in health policymaking", *Research Evaluation*, Vol. 25/3, pp. 315-328, http://dx.doi.org/10.1093/reseval/rvv044. [4]

Robinson, E. (2017), *Family Matters - Issue 99 - The Expert Panel Project | Australian Institute of Family Studies*, https://aifs.gov.au/publications/family-matters/issue-99/expert-panel-project (accessed on 5 September 2018). [34]

Rushmer, R., D. Hunter and A. Steven (2014), "Using interactive workshops to prompt knowledge exchange: a realist evaluation of a knowledge to action initiative", *Public Health*, Vol. 128/6, pp. 552-560, http://dx.doi.org/10.1016/J.PUHE.2014.03.012. [25]

Shaxson, L. (2019), "Uncovering the practices of evidence-informed policy-making", *Public Money & Management*, Vol. 39/1, pp. 46-55, http://dx.doi.org/10.1080/09540962.2019.1537705. [46]

Shroff, Z. et al. (2015), "Incorporating research evidence into decision-making processes: researcher and decision-maker perceptions from five low- and middle-income countries", *Health Research Policy and Systems*, Vol. 13/1, p. 70, http://dx.doi.org/10.1186/s12961-015-0059-y. [8]

SITRA (2017), *Hack for Society - Sitra*, https://www.sitra.fi/en/projects/hack-for-society/#what-is-it-about (accessed on 6 February 2019). [35]

SITRA (2017), *Public-sector leadership training - Sitra*, https://www.sitra.fi/en/projects/public-sector-leadership-training/ (accessed on 6 February 2019). [16]

Stewart, R., L. Langer and Y. Erasmus (2018), "An integrated model for increasing the use of evidence by decision-makers for improved development", *Development Southern Africa*, pp. 1-16, http://dx.doi.org/10.1080/0376835X.2018.1543579. [26]

Taylor, R. et al. (2004), "Critical appraisal skills training for health care professionals: a randomized controlled trial [ISRCTN46272378]", *BMC Medical Education*, Vol. 4/1, p. 30, http://dx.doi.org/10.1186/1472-6920-4-30. [24]

U.S. Department of Veterans Affairs (2017), *Overview - Partnered Evidence-Based Policy Resource Center*, https://www.peprec.research.va.gov/PEPRECRESEARCH/overview.asp (accessed on 4 March 2019). [38]

University of Wisconsin-Madison (2019), *National Poverty Research Center*, https://www.irp.wisc.edu/national-poverty-research-center/ (accessed on 4 March 2019). [37]

Washington, S. and M. Mintrom (2018), "Strengthening policy capability: New Zealand's Policy Project", *Policy Design and Practice*, Vol. 1/1, pp. 30-46, http://dx.doi.org/10.1080/25741292.2018.1425086. [45]

Wehrens, R., M. Bekker and R. Bal (2010), "The construction of evidence-based local health policy through partnerships: Research infrastructure, process, and context in the Rotterdam 'Healthy in the City' programme", *Journal of Public Health Policy*, Vol. 31/4, pp. 447-460, http://dx.doi.org/10.1057/jphp.2010.33. [36]

What Works Network (2018), *The Rise of Experimental Government: Cross-Government Trial Advice Panel Update Report*, https://assets.publishing.service.gov.uk/government/uploads/system/uploads/attachment_data/file/753468/RiseExperimentalGovernment_Cross-GovTrialAdvicePanelUpdateReport.pdf (accessed on 24 January 2019). [33]

Wilsdon, J., M. Saner and P. Gluckman (2018), "INGSA Manifesto for 2030: Science Advice for Global Goals", INGSA, http://dx.doi.org/10.1057/palcomms.2016.77. [21]

Note

[1] As with any categorisation exercise, it is recognised that any one intervention could belong in more than one category.

5 Conclusion

This closing chapter draws the lessons of the analysis of the skills and other contributing factors to evidence-informed policy-making. It offers a number of recommendations to make the use of evidence more effective, including the need to be aware of the local and political context, the need to address the full range of skills and capacities. The recommendations also highlight the institutional and organisational structures and systems that enable effective use of evidence, as well as the role of strategic leadership and the need to embed evaluation from the beginning to inform the implementation process. The chapter also highlights potential areas for future work, including a professional development framework, as well as the need to address the impact of cognitive and motivational aspects of capacity building.

Increasing governments' capacity for an evidence-informed approach to policy-making that is fully able to make use of policy evaluation within the public sector, is a critical part of fostering good public governance. Based on the evidence that was gathered, this report calls for investing in individual skills for the use of evidence by senior policy-makers and for building capacity for evidence-informed policy-making at a systemic and organisational level.

The goal is to enable agile and responsive government, which is well equipped to address complex and at times "wicked" policy challenges, in a shifting political environment, driven by short-term political pressures and conflicting voices. Evidence has a critical role to play in responding to these challenges, by improving the capacity of government to shape effective public policies and deliver quality, responsiveness and accessibility of public services. Evidence can play a role throughout the key stages of the policy cycle and is increasingly recognised as a critical part of good governance.

Despite the potential for policies to be based on evidence, an effective connection between the supply and the demand for evidence in the policy-making process remains often elusive. Many governments lack the necessary infrastructure to build effective connections between evidence and decision-making. Although civil servants may have access to evidence and acknowledge the importance of using it, many do not use it systematically in crafting policy analysis. Furthermore, policy-makers experience a range of other barriers to accessing timely and relevant evidence. While a single solution and tool may not exist for each of these challenges, there is value for countries in building capacity for policy-making at the systemic and strategic level.

This report presents the interventions; tools and strategies governments can use to build their capacity for an evidence-informed approach that fully leverages the value of evidence for policy-making. It also leverages a skills framework that was jointly elaborated with the EU/JRC. These include: diagnostic tools to understand the range of existing capacities and ensuring that interventions are well matched to governments' needs; initiatives designed to increase policymakers' ability to access and obtain evidence; initiatives to improve individual policymaker's capacity to use evidence; mentoring to provide personalised guidance in relation to 'real-world' application of knowledge, and strategies for promoting interaction and engagement between researchers and policy-makers.

The use of evidence is also intimately linked to organisational structures and systems. Improving organisational capacity includes a range of strategies such as improving organisational infrastructure; improving organisational tools, resources and processes; workforce development; and establishing strategic units to support an evidence-informed approach.

Recommendations

In addition to highlighting good practices for enhancing the collective skill set in the public sector, the report offers a framework that countries can use to identify and select interventions, tools and strategies to build their capacity for an evidence-informed approach. The following five key conclusions are designed to maximise the value countries can expect in using this framework:

1. **Capacity building initiatives need to be aware of the local political and institutional context of research use.**

Without an understanding of how policy-makers engage with research evidence and how they integrate it with other forms of input into the policy-making process, capacity-building initiatives risk being poorly aligned to the local context and culture. In reality, many initiatives have insufficient knowledge of the local practice and context that they are trying to address. Creating capacity-building initiatives that reflect the local needs and context therefore requires generating an understanding of the messy reality of how actual policy-making occurs and what are the opportunities for evidence to play a role. For example, in a government that has civil servants who have all the capabilities to use evidence, but not the motivation, nor opportunity to do so, implementing a generic skills training exercise in isolation is unlikely to effective. The diagnostic tools identified in this report therefore have an important role to play in helping governments understand their current context of evidence use and what range of strategies are necessary to improve their capacity for EIPM. This can be particularly important as governments are facing citizens' concerns and a lack of trust in public institutions.

2. **Capacity building initiatives need to address the full range of skills and capacities that influence the use of evidence, including skills for understanding, obtaining, interrogating and assessing, using and applying evidence, as well as engaging with stakeholders and evaluating success.**

Developing capacity for the use of evidence requires consideration of the current capacities within the system, spanning the individual and the organisational levels. A key first step for policy organisations, which are unclear about what their current capacities, are: first, to gather information on the range of current capacities; second, to foster the desire for change; and third, to identify the barriers and facilitators of evidence use within the system. Following a gap analysis, organisations can use the skills framework of this report to identify the right kind of skills and leverage some of the examples that are offered.

3. **Institutional and organisational structures and systems enable the effective use of evidence – without addressing these, change initiatives are unlikely to succeed.**

Building individual skills and capacity are critical components of strategies to improve the use of evidence. However, a sole focus on individuals limits the potential to engender long-term and system-wide change, especially in the context of the rotation of employees experienced in the civil service, whether as a result of regular rotations or related to a change of government. This means that building the civil service's capacity to improve the use of evidence necessitates consideration of the institutional elements that can support this. This report has reviewed a range of organisational strategies that show promise, including: strengthening organisational tools, resources and processes; making investments in basic infrastructure; and establishing strategic units to support an evidence-informed approach. *Mandates, legislation and regulation are also important tools to facilitate the use of evidence.*

4. **Strategic leadership is critical to drive the organisational change necessary for improved evidence-informed policy-making.**

Strategic and committed leadership is a crucial driver for the change needed to embed an evidence-informed approach to policy-making. Public sector senior civil leadership programmes can help to support senior leaders to face the current challenges of public administration and enable leadership of the evidence agenda. Using high profile positions as a catalyst is another strategy for creating the necessary momentum for driving change in policy settings. These can include senior positions such as Chief Economists, Chief Information Officers, Chief Evaluation Officers and Chief Science Advisors. An evidence-informed approach can also be leveraged through performance-driven approaches to resource allocation. For example, accountability tools can be used to incentivise EIPM by the senior civil service. This can then help to promote the use of evidence throughout public sector organisations: if the senior civil service are held to account for the quality of the evidence base they use to make policy proposals and decisions with, then they will implement measures to ensure that the rest of the organisation is incentivised to use evidence, such as by including evidence use in the civil service competency framework.

5. **Capacity building initiatives should embed evaluation from the beginning to inform the implementation process and support continuous learning and improvement.**

Evaluating the impact of capacity building interventions should be a priority for governments embarking on initiatives. This is critical to ensure governments do not waste resources on ineffective or inefficient interventions. Despite the increased interest in stimulating demand for evidence and a number of reviews of the effectiveness of different initiatives to do so (Langer, Tripney and Gough, 2016[1]; Haynes et al., 2018[2]), there remains a paucity of evaluations of the impact of interventions. This knowledge gap is especially noticeable in relation to initiatives targeting organisational processes, resources and tools – and so building in rigorous evaluation should be a priority.

6. **Capacity building initiatives need to be embedded within organisational structures and strategies to enable sustainability and long-term change.**

Evidence-informed policy-making is unlikely to become integrated into the 'business as usual' operation of policy organisations as a result of short term and short-lived initiatives. There is a need for continuous involvement and exposure to capacity building initiatives by embedding these into existing work and organisational structures and systems. Greater consideration of these opportunities for organisational learning should reduce the risk that initiatives get 'washed out' after an initial period of enthusiasm. Strategies to promote sustainability can include legislative approaches as well as departmental evidence strategies. A consistent message across the reviewed initiatives is that increasing capacity for evidence use is a long term and evolving process. This means often starting with manageable initiatives and building from there, whilst being realistic about when expected results will materialise.

Future work

The analysis contained in this report can offer opportunities for follow up work:

- *Developing a continuous professional development framework:* The framework would also need to specify which individuals within a given context require which skills in order to contribute towards an evidence-informed approach. For example, elected officials can play an important role in creating demand for evidence and creating a culture of evidence use within Ministries. This continuous professional development could be offered at various stages, including senior and junior level. The Senior Civil Service also plays a critical role in policy development, and may remain in post longer than elected officials. Therefore, supporting the Senior Civil Service to build their capacity can help deliver results in the long term. Alternatively, investing in more junior levels may also represent an investment in the future, and junior members may also have significant responsibility in shaping and drafting policy proposals from the start at the inception phase.

- *Collecting examples of initiatives from a wider range of policy areas and countries.* This report benefited from a significant range of expertise and grey literature, as well as engagement with OECD stakeholders. Nevertheless, it could be further enriched by more in-depth country examples. Delegates will be invited to submit any additional information to enrich the findings and analysis of the report, particularly across linguistic boundaries for countries where the information is more difficult to identify.

- *Further addressing the impact of cognitive and motivational aspects of capacity building.* One takeaway from the reviews of interventions included in this report e.g. (Langer, Tripney and Gough, 2016[1]; Haynes et al., 2018[2]) is that interventions to improve evidence-informed policy-making need to be based on sound programme logic and the best available evidence. While this report helps to consolidate policy-making process through improved facts and policy evaluations, addressing more fully the cognitive dimension might be helpful in the future. The role of self-interest can also be very important. The role of memory bias, information asymmetries, aversion to risk and bias in perception might play an important role in skewing policy outcomes. It might be useful to create opportunities for the policy-making process to become aware of the potential impact of such biases to at least ensure that decisions are taken in a full information environment. Some of the work conducted by the EU JRC as part of its Enlightenment 2.0 project[1] and the pilot project "Science meets Parliaments / Science meets Regions" might also be very relevant in this respect. Similarly, there is further scope to investigate the motivational and cultural factors necessary to generate a culture of EIPM in the civil service, which could benefit from further OECD work on public employment and management.

References

Haynes, A. et al. (2018), "What can we learn from interventions that aim to increase policy-makers' capacity to use research? A realist scoping review", *Health Research Policy and Systems*, Vol. 16/1, p. 31, http://dx.doi.org/10.1186/s12961-018-0277-1. [2]

Langer, L., J. Tripney and D. Gough (2016), *The science of using science: researching the use of Research evidence in decision-making.*. [1]

Note

[1] https://ec.europa.eu/jrc/en/enlightenment-research-programme.

Annex A. Mapping of interventions, strategies and tools onto the skills framework for EIPM

Skill	Definition	Types of Interventions	Examples of Interventions
Understanding	Policy makers with this skill will understand the role of evidence and its place in the policy making cycle, as well as the challenges and opportunities which come with the use of evidence. This will be underpinned by knowledge of different research methods and their purpose, as well as the fundamentals of statistical and data literacy (including big data, machine learning and artificial intelligence).	Diagnostic tools of individual capacity: Used to determine individual capacity and motivation to use evidence in their work.	Australia's Staff Assessment of enGagement with Evidence (SAGE) – a tool that aims to provide an evaluation of current levels of research engagement and use. SAGE combines an interview and document analysis to concretely assess how policy makers engaged with research, how research was used and what barriers impacted the use of research in relation to a specific policy product.
			Australia's Seeking, Engaging with and Evaluating Research (SEER) – a practical tool that assists policy agencies in assessing their capacity to use research, and evaluates the success of initiatives designed to improve evidence use in policy making.
		Senior Civil Service programmes: These programmes work to encourage senior civil servants to use evidence and trains the senior civil service in how to create a culture within their organisations of evidence use.	Finland's Public Sector Leadership training – a programme that strengthens the ability of public-sector leaders to handle challenges and support the public sector in the reform of its social role.
Obtaining	Policy makers with this skill be able to gather existing evidence in their own policy area and know who to turn to as sources of evidence synthesis. They will be able to recognise where there are evidence gaps and commission high quality evidence to fill these gaps using a range of project management techniques.	Access to research through online databases: Providing policy makers with access to research articles or syntheses via an online database aims to maximise access to specific types of research and increase policy makers' confidence in accessing and using such content.	Campbell Collaboration – promotes positive social and economic change through the production and use of systematic reviews and other evidence synthesis for evidence-informed policy and practice.
			Cochrane Library – is global independent network of researchers, professionals, patients, carers and people interested in health. The Cochrane Library contains systematic reviews of medical and healthcare interventions.
		Disseminating tailored syntheses of evidence: Increasing the ease of access through having relevant research evidence synthesized, tailored for specific users and sent directly to policy makers, in order to increase policy makers' use of evidence.	Argentina's Health Policy Research briefs – the WHO runs a programme where they product policy briefs for policy makers on research evidence tailored to the policy makers' needs.
			UK What Works Centres produce a range of policy briefs to disseminate key messages to its target audience, including policy makers.
		Commissioning research and reviews:	UK's Policy Reviews Facility – a place where policy teams, government analysts and academic experts from three

Skill	Definition	Types of Interventions	Examples of Interventions
		Ensuring policy makers are able to commission evidence when there is gaps in the research. This can lead to policy makers increasing their engagement with and control of the research which in turn would increase the relevance and applicability of the research.	universities work closely together to determine the focus of systematic review products to best meet the needs of policy work.
			Australia's 'Evidence Check' – assists Australian policy makers in commissioning high quality reviews of research with knowledge brokers who assist to formulate and refine the scope of and questions addressed by the review.
			The US's Office of Management and Budget has developed grant review and support structures to assess the quality of evidence being commissioned by policy makers and government agencies.
		Seminars to present research findings Presenting policy makers with relevant research. Seminars are generally well received by participants and preferred to reading reports by many.	The Joint Research Centre's lunchtime science lecture series – The seminars features JRC scientists and researchers, as well as external guest speakers. The seminars are also web streamed so participants can join from anywhere.
Interrogating and Assessing	Policy makers with this skill will make use of a set of holistic, systemic and critical thinking tools. They will be able to assess the provenance, reliability and appropriateness of evidence. They will have an ability to interrogate evidence by critically assessing its quality and context, using a range of techniques to challenge assumptions and biases.	Intensive skills training programmes: Increasing policy makers' capacity to engage with and understand the more technical sides of research findings. Training programmes can be very effective when they are learner centred and participatory, ideally embedded within long-term strategies for professional development.	INGSA's capacity building initiatives – a collaborative platform for policy exchange, capacity building and research across diverse global science advisory organisations and national systems. The initiative provides workshops, conferences, tools and guidance.
			The UK's Alliance for Useful Evidence – runs an Evidence Masterclass where policy makers can learn about how to use evidence in their policy work and can practice their new skills through simulations.
		Knowledge brokers (organisations) Knowledge brokers can help to facilitate policymakers' access to research evidence by helping them to navigate research material that may be unfamiliar.	Poland's Centre for Evaluation and Analysis of Public Policies – a research centre that is part of a university. The Centre aims to work together with public administration in the field of evaluation and analysis of public policies, and its methodology.
			Top Institute of Evidence-Based Education Research in the Netherlands – a research centre belonging to an academic institution. The Centre produces research for policy makers to use in their work.
			Australian Institute for Family Studies (AIFS) – a government agency in the Department of Social Services. Fills the knowledge broker function while being within the government.
			The Research and Evaluation Unit Department of Children and Youth Affair in Ireland – working within the government as a knowledge broker unit, providing evidence to the government Department.
			The Haut Conseil à l'Enfance, la Famille et l'Âge in France – the Department integrates knowledge broker functions into its day-to-day operations.

Skill	Definition	Types of Interventions	Examples of Interventions
Using and Applying	Policy makers with this skill will understand their own policy context and recognise possible uses of evidence in the policy cycle. They will be proficient in knowledge management and understand the role of innovation, with an ability to assess and manage risks and challenges. They will be familiar with and know when to use innovative techniques like behavioural insights, design thinking, policy labs and foresight.	Intensive skills training programmes: Training programmes geared towards policy makers can provide them with the necessary skills to increase the use of evidence in their work. Training programmes can be very effective when they are learner centred and participatory, ideally embedded within long-term strategies for professional development.	OECD/Mexico's Capacity Building for RIA – in partnership with the OECD, Mexico's Ministry of Economy hosted a four day seminar of how to produce and analyse impact assessments.
			In Canada, the Executive Training in Research Application (EXTRA) programme – provides support and development for leaders in using research. Participants learn how to use evidence in their decision making and are then able to train their co-workers.
			Public Sector Training in Finland – SITRA, the Finnish Innovation Fund has a programme for policy makers to increase their skills and capacity in their role, which includes a module on putting new practices and lessons learned from experiments into practice.
			Portugal's National Institute of Public Administration – on an annual basis, all public service organisations inform the National Institute of Public Administration of employees' training needs, which then feeds into the development of an annual training programme.
			UK's Behavioural Insights Team – runs many trials across the world related to increasing knowledge of behavioural insights, which are accompanied with corresponding capacity building of local civil servants.
		Knowledge brokers (individuals): Individuals as knowledge brokers can present relevant research directly to policy makers. Many governments have official positions like Chief Science Advisor whose role is to present evidence to parliament.	New Zealand's Chief Science Advisors – the Government has Chief Science Advisors for both the Prime Minister and the Cabinet as well as individual Ministries. They work to improve the use of evidence in policy development and provide advice.
			In the UK, the Government Chief Science Advisor's (GCSA) role is to advise the Prime Minister and Cabinet on science, engineering and technology. The GCSA reports directly to the Cabinet Secretary and works closely with the Science Minister, and other ministers and permanent secretaries across Whitehall.
			In Australia, the GCSA advises the Prime Minister and Cabinet, and also holds the position of Executive Officer of the Commonwealth Science Council to identify challenges and opportunities for Australia that can be addressed using science.
		Mentoring: Mentoring can provide policy makers individualised training where they can learn the skills from their peers and ask questions and get feedback on using evidence in their work.	South Africa's mentoring programme for policy makers – through this programme, policy makers are trained in evidence use and then are paired up with colleagues who have not received training in order to mentor them one-on-one.

Skill	Definition	Types of Interventions	Examples of Interventions
Engaging with Stakeholders	Policy makers with this skill will have strong engagement and communication skills, including ability to create effective evidence based messages for different types of audiences and to engage and inspire variety of stakeholders. They will be able to manage and facilitate evidence-informed debate with policy makers and citizens, and maintain collaboration with the evidence community. They will have a good grasp of co-creation, co-production and participatory methodologies.	One-off or periodic interactive forums: Interventions and approaches that bring together policy makers and researchers. This approach aims to build mutual interest, trust, respect as well as promoting learning about each other's values, contexts, constraints and practices.	Joint Research Centre's Evidence and policy summer school – aims to help junior to mid-career policy makers to use evidence for policy solutions. The summer school focuses on the tools and approaches to inform the policy making process through evidence.
			Australian Primary Health Care Research Institute (APHCRI) 'Conversations' – which is a regular programme of roundtable presentations held at the Department of Health to facilitate exchange between APHCRI Network researchers and Department policy makers.
		Platforms for ongoing interactivity: Platforms for ongoing interactivity can include communities of practice, formal networks and cross sector committees. Repeated face to face contact permits the development of trust, respect and ease of communication between policy makers and stakeholders.	The Global Preventing Violence Across the Lifespan Network (PreVAil) – an integrated knowledge translation network to support effective partnerships between its members as well as joint research and application in the area of family violence prevention.
			Policy Liaison Initiative for improving the use of Cochrane systematic reviews – an 'Evidence-Based Policy Network' that facilitates knowledge sharing between policy makers and researchers, alongside seminars by national and international researchers in the field of evidence synthesis and implementation.
		Partnership projects: Partnership projects include various schemes to bring policy makers into contact with individual scientists, through collaborating in the development of research projects.	The Netherlands Academic Collaborative Centres – a virtual infrastructure for long-term collaborations between a regional Public Health Service (PHS) and a university research department.
			UK Pairing Programme – links policy makers with a range of experts through 'Policy Fellowships'. The programme aims to facilitate more dialogue between the two communities, to make research more accessible, and to increase policy makers' use of evidence in their work.
			The Australian Institute of Family Studies (AIFS) – a government body that has developed an 'Expert Panel' which gathers experts in research, practice and evaluation, who support practitioners in the implementation of policies, measuring outcomes, trying new policy approaches and conducting research and evaluations.
			Finland's 'Hack for Society' – brings together academics, NGOs as well as national and local government to develop co-creative teams to work on service design, co-creation and societal trials.
			In the US, The National Poverty Research Center – a partnership between the US Department of Health and Human Services and the University of Wisconsin-Madison, providing research, training and

Skill	Definition	Types of Interventions	Examples of Interventions
			dissemination to inform policy and practice.
			The US' Quality Enhancement Research Initiative –provides timely, rigorous data analysis to the government to support the development of policy by bringing together stakeholders including practitioners, researchers, policy makers, service users and the general public to inform research and policy recommendations.
Evaluating	Policy makers with this skill will understand different evaluation approaches and tools, and know how to use comparative examples to inform EIPM. They will understand that evaluation should be built in the policy cycle and should serve to inform and improve EIPM. They will know and use qualitative and quantitative indicators of successful evidence use.	Diagnostic tools of organisational capacity for evidence use: Diagnostic tools can measure organisation's capacity to access, interpret and use research findings in order to identify strengths, areas for improvement and assess the impact of capacity building initiatives.	Canada's Evidence Literacy diagnostic tool – a self-assessment tool to help service managers and policy organisations understand their capacity to acquire assess, adapt and apply research
			The US's 'Norm of Evidence and Research in Decision-making' (NERD) – a tool that can be used across organizational and functional settings to assess evidence based management practices within an agency.
			Organisational Research Access, Culture and Leadership (ORACLe) – a tool that assesses multiple dimensions of organisational capacity including the systems, supports and tools that organisations have in place to use research, as well as the values placed on research within an organisation.